What do you do when . . .

- Your daughter is sobbing because her BFF betrayed her?
- Your teen withdraws and won't talk?
- A loved one gets seriously ill or passes away?
- Your ex doesn't show up for a promised event?
- Your son is bullied for being "different"?
- You find out your teen is sexually active?
- Your 13-year-old, 115-pound daughter thinks she's too fat and needs to diet?
- Your son takes out his anger at not making the football team on your walls and furniture?
- A mean comment about your child pops up on social media?
- Your son says you'd be better off without him?
- Your oldest says she hates you and wants to go live with her father?

These are just a few situations you may face as a parent. Your kid's world is so different from the one you grew up in. A lot more scary on many fronts too. So when your children hurt, how can you best help them?

When Your Kid Is Hurting walks you through real-life issues, your child's fears and hurts, and natural coping mechanisms for stress and grief. With some of my time-tested advice that has worked for hundreds of thousands of families, you and your child can not only get through these difficult experiences intact but also develop a deeper bond and healthy perspective that will serve you well in the future.

I guarantee it.

When
Your Kid
Is
Hurting

When
Your Kid
Is
Hurting

Helping Your Child
through the Tough Days

Dr. Kevin Leman

Revell

a division of Baker Publishing Group
Grand Rapids, Michigan

© 2018 by Dr. Kevin Leman

Published by Revell
a division of Baker Publishing Group
PO Box 6287, Grand Rapids, MI 49516-6287
www.revellbooks.com

Printed in the United States of America

Library of Congress Cataloging-in-Publication Data
Names: Leman, Kevin, author.
Title: When your kid is hurting : helping your child through the tough days / Dr. Kevin Leman.
Description: Grand Rapids, MI : Revell, a division of Baker Publishing Group, [2018] | Includes bibliographical references and index.
Identifiers: LCCN 2018007096 | ISBN 9780800723064 (cloth : alk. paper)
Subjects: LCSH: Parent and child—Religious aspects—Christianity. | Parenting—Religious aspects—Christianity. | Child rearing—Religious aspects—Christianity. | Child psychology. | Consolation.
Classification: LCC BV4529 .L46 2018 | DDC 248.8/45—dc23
LC record available at https://lccn.loc.gov/2018007096

ISBN 978-0-8007-3506-7 (ITPE)

To protect the privacy of those who have shared their stories with the author, some details and names have been changed.

19   20   21   22   23   24   7   6   5   4   3   2

For all those who have been hurt by life.

May the words of this book be used by those who love you much more than you know to encourage you.

CONTENTS

ACKNOWLEDGMENTS

Grateful thanks to:

My longtime Revell team.

My editor and friend Ramona Tucker, for understanding my passion for helping hurting kids and walking with me on that journey.

INTRODUCTION

As the World Squirms

It's not your grandmama's world, and it's not yours either. Times have greatly changed.

Your kids are growing up in a world very different from the one you grew up in.

But you don't need me to tell you that because you experience reminders of that truth every day. Today's world is fast-paced, tumultuous, competitive, and violent at times. Even if you're a young parent in your twenties, a lot has changed since you graduated from high school. Just think about the first computer and cell phone you owned. Then take a look at all the technological devices you own now and what they can do.

The intensity of that pace deeply affects your child, even on her good days. That's why bad days and difficult experiences can be particularly traumatic if your child doesn't have the tools to deal with such events.

Children today face multiple issues simultaneously. As much as you might try to cushion them, they are forced to grow up more swiftly as they are assaulted by information and events on all sides. I group those real-life issues into two categories—what is "out there" and what is "in here." Here's what I mean.

We live in a violent world, with shootings in schools and on city streets, racial violence, terrorism, and cyber-slandering. Your kids face those types of "out there" contemporary issues—the events every human is aware of because of the society we live in. Due to the bombardment of media, today's children are more aware of those types of events than previous generations. With a few clicks of a mouse or swipes on a smartphone, they can be connected to the gravity and terror of those situations—without parental guidance or the tools to deal with what they see and hear.

The result? Either they are traumatized and approach life more fearfully, or they become anesthetized to the hurts of others and unable to grapple with their own. Neither option is good long-term.

Your kids also face "in here" issues—relational and personal issues that hit them between the eyes psychologically, emotionally, and physically. That includes parents splitting up, getting shuffled between houses, and having MIA dads or moms. You might be the aunt or grandparent they currently live with. Dealing with court issues and the legal system is a way of life they accept as normal.

When I was growing up, I only knew one kid whose parents were divorced. That kid felt he stuck out like a sore thumb among all the other two-parent families. Fast-forward to today, where many kids have last names that are different from their siblings or the parent they currently live with. Many parents have divorced or never married. Kids might be raised in a single-parent home or live with a guardian.

Children also deal with depression and the death of loved ones through cancer, accident, and suicide. They are betrayed by friends and encounter bullying and cyber-bullying. They are told they are stupid, fat, or "the wrong color." They can become the prey of sexual predators and power-hungry, need-to-be-in-control individuals.

Yes, we can and should teach our kids how to protect themselves. For example, we can teach them basic self-defense skills and about "stranger danger." But what do you do if the real danger comes from within? Most physical, sexual, and verbal abuse happens within the family or extended family. And what if your child innocently releases details about herself, her location, and her habits on the internet and is targeted by vindictive peers or an online stalker?

How do you respond when your daughter's friend commits suicide? A BFF gossips about her? She ends up pregnant? Your deployed spouse is killed in action and your son says he wants to die too?

How do you react when your son is devastated because he didn't make the team and he won't talk to you about it? When your daughter refuses to eat because someone called her "chunky"?

In such situations and many others, how can you keep your child's heart and mind protected from long-term damage that could affect their self-worth and relationships in the future?

It's critical that parents help kids find new ways to process information and feelings in a healthy manner. Such an approach isn't merely about coping; it allows them to grow in their understanding of life and its realities. It will put them firmly on the path of becoming an adult who can give back to the world, rather than one who lashes out against others in retribution or retreats to live in a shell in fear.

When Your Kid Is Hurting will help you navigate these real-life "out there" and "in here" issues; understand your child's world, experiences, and fears; and learn how your child grieves. You'll discover how to walk through negative experiences with a healthy, balanced perspective that will hone your skills and your child's to handle not only these events but ones that may occur down the road.

Here are just a few of the topics we'll explore in this book:

- How can you know what your child is really thinking?
- How can you talk in a way he'll want to listen, even if he's seemingly shut you out?
- What's the best way to acknowledge her hurt? What should you say and not say? Do and not do?
- How can you address this particular event without making her feel further like a victim?
- How do you know if his behavior is normal or if professional help is needed?
- If a loved one is ill, how much should you tell your child? What if he can't handle it?
- What's the best way to support your child during a tough time?
- Where's that fine line between protecting and overprotecting your child?
- When should you step into a situation with peers, and when should you butt out?
- How can you turn this trauma into a teachable moment that will benefit him in the future?
- What's the best way to guide her through this negative experience? To help her get up again when she's been knocked down?

The first couple of chapters will walk you through an overview of the biggest "out there" and "in here" issues that today's kids and parents face. You'll learn practical ways to respond to your child's questions, hurts, and concerns.

Chapter 3 addresses the basic fears every child has and the antidotes within your control.

In chapter 4 we'll talk about why kids grieve differently and what their behavior means.

In chapter 5 you'll discover how your child views herself so you can connect on her level.

Chapter 6 reveals three distinctive types of parents and how their approaches affect their hurting kids, so you can identify and then adapt your own style if needed.

In chapter 7 you'll learn the best moves to turn your child's traumas into a game plan that will benefit her in the future when other tough situations arise (and they will—that's just life!).

No parent likes to see their child hurting. That's why I've provided a hefty "Ask Dr. Leman" section as your armchair companion. It includes the hottest questions parents ask me all the time and my time-tested answers. Even if the specific situations described aren't quite a match to yours, the principles and suggestions I give for the topic should be helpful to you.

If you don't find an answer that relates to your area of concern, feel free to shoot me your question on Facebook (www.facebook.com/DrKevinLeman), and I'd be honored to help you. If you're wondering about it, likely so are hundreds or thousands of other parents.

The game of life isn't always easy to master. If you're reading this book, it's likely your child is undergoing a surprise twist that neither of you expected. *When Your Kid Is Hurting* will show you how to walk through that negative event in ways that will shape your child into a resilient, positive, and competent person you're proud to call your son or daughter.

1

"Out There" Issues

How you can respond practically to your child's
fears about real-world problems.

We live in a violent world. Tragic events that happen in our country and around the world confirm that bad things do happen . . . even to good people. Mass shootings, racial and gender discrimination, gang violence, terrorism, diseases like the Ebola virus, abuse, suicide attempts, and bullying are only a few of the sad realities in today's world.

When we as parents see these seemingly senseless events occur, our natural protectiveness makes us want to batten down the hatches and keep our kids close to our side 24/7. If we do that, we think, they'll be safe. However, such an action isn't humanly possible. (Plus, for a growing number of parents, violence occurs within their own home, which should be a safe zone.)

So how do we deal with these big issues "out there" that we have absolutely no control over, such as a random shooting?

Have you ever seen a little child who is scared of an imaginary monster under his bed? What does he usually do? He covers his eyes. *If I can't see it,* he reasons, *then it doesn't exist and it can't scare me.*

Some parents have an MA in denial. Those who use this approach hide their heads in the sand to deny that violent events can happen in their sphere. They persist in thinking, *We live in a small town. Nothing like that will happen here. Our kids are safe.* But then the unimaginable does happen, like the tragedy at Sandy Hook Elementary School, and parents and children aren't equipped to deal with it.

Other parents play Mama Hen, drawing their chicks under their wings and not allowing them to cohabit with the chicks of other flocks. Problem is, those chicks can't stay under Mama's wings forever. What happens when they're on their own and they have to live in the larger world?

There's a better way. It starts with being informed and aware.

Today's Big Issues

There are numerous "out there" issues that negatively impact children as they grow up in today's society. In this section, I'll give you a bird's-eye overview of the biggest ones that parents say keep them up at night.

The Pervasive Influence of Media and Social Media

Television, movies, "real-life" dramas, and social media sensationalize violence, sex, destructive acts, and death, desensitizing viewers to what death truly is and how grief and loss really affect someone in the short term and long term.

This "Hollywood experience" sets up in young minds unrealistic expectations about what life should be like—a party 24/7, with plenty of booze, sex, and a morning-after pill to solve any unwanted side effects. Even harmful, vicious, dangerous acts aren't serious. They can be undone by clicking a back arrow on a screen. There is no accountability or responsibility.

Why else would an 18-year-old, as reported in the news, drive under the influence while simultaneously livestreaming on Instagram, with her 14-year-old sister and her sister's friend in the car? When the car spun out of control, the 14-year-old sister was ejected from the car and killed. A viewer's captured footage shows the driver singing along to music, then panning the phone to capture the image of her sister's dead body by the side of the road. All she could think of to say was, "This is the last thing I wanted to happen."[1]

To many kids, life is like viewing a movie. *It isn't real.*

Yes, likely other issues were going on in that 18-year-old's life, but how do you explain a teenager unemotionally recording an image like that? The callousness of such an act is astounding and horrifying.

So is the fact that a group of teens filmed a disabled man drowning and did nothing to help him. As he disappeared under the water, one of the teens simply said, "Oh, he just died." The teens, between 14 and 16 years old, didn't even call 911 to report the drowning.[2]

Truth is, the bombardment of media and social media has served to further distance our kids from reality rather than make them more aware of and able to deal with it. To many kids, life is like viewing a movie. *It isn't real.*

For example, when actors die in a movie, they come back to life for the next movie. But that girl's sister won't. Nor will the man who drowned.

Also, the prevalence of intense emotion in social media anesthetizes children to pain. They expect violence and death in video games and movies. Without it, there's not enough action. After all, being successful is all about getting more views on YouTube and more likes on Facebook. The overabundance and ease of accessing harsh images leads to bland, uncaring children who don't understand real-life pain or have the tools to cope with difficulties when bad things happen to them.

Most news reports also err on the side of sensationalism. They cover and hype everything bad, leading kids to believe that there's nothing good in the world anymore. Not as much news focuses on the inspirational acts of heroes—people you'd want your kids to emulate. A saturation of negative news can't help but produce negativity in the generations that consume it.

Children are also assaulted with unrealistic body images through magazines, movies, Instagram, Facebook, and tabloids about their favorite stars. What average teenage girl wouldn't feel inadequate stacked up to a Victoria's Secret lingerie model? And if what it takes to get a girl to like you and want to sleep with you is drinking the right kind of beer or vodka, what teenage boy would think twice about paying for a fake ID?

With the overemphasis on sex, today's kids are sexting more than ever before. They are also seeing many images that aren't age-appropriate. For example, your first grader, who loves kitty cats, is searching the internet for cute pictures. All of a sudden she sees a heading that makes her think she's about to view some of her best friend little creatures. She clicks on the heading and sees . . . well, not exactly what she expected. There's an image she doesn't quite know how to interpret, yet it's imprinted on her brain forever. If you don't believe me, ask a guy you know if he's ever seen any pornography. Ninety-nine out of 100 guys will say yes. Ask him if he can recall when the first time was. Chances are, he can tell you exactly. Once shocking images like that hit our brain, they are embedded in there forever.

That's why I urge parents to be careful about giving smartphones to young children and to be watchful of their internet access. Kids today might be more aware, but they still deserve a childhood.

What can you do about this new Goliath? Technology and media are here to stay. You're fighting an uphill, ridiculous battle if you try to disregard them. It's humanly impossible to escape such negative images yourself or to withhold them from your children. So how can you teach your kids to handle them in a positive manner, making discerning choices? How much should you control what influences your kids, and how much should you simply play the role of guide as they explore various aspects of media?

Kids today might be more aware, but they still deserve a childhood.

So much of what your child views and the way she interprets that information has to do with what she experiences at home. The type of relationship she has with you can make all the difference. Is it open, caring, and nonjudgmental? If so, she'll be much more likely to share with you what she's viewing.

Mass Shootings on the Rise

Our nation is getting angrier. In 2012, 28 people died—20 of them grade-school children—in the Sandy Hook Elementary School massacre. In mass shootings in 2013, 5 people were killed in Santa Monica, California, and another 12 in Washington, DC. In 2014, 3 were killed in Fort Hood, Texas, and another 6 in Isla Vista, California. In 2015 there were 5 mass shootings, with 40 people dead. In 2016, 50 people were killed at a nightclub. It was the deadliest mass shooting in US history. In April 2017, a man opened fire inside an elementary school in San Bernardino, California, killing 3 people, including an 8-year-old boy and himself.[3]

Schools, churches, shopping malls, clubs—places that were once considered safe—are facing shock waves of fallout after these types of events. Random shootings can happen anytime, anywhere, causing untold damage. Innocent children who are simply walking down a street can be caught in the middle of gunfire.

Yes, your school can install protective devices. They can provide crisis training sessions for students, teachers, and administration with the local PD or SWAT. But no device or training can completely stop an angry person from wreaking revenge on an unsuspecting world because he's not happy with the way life is treating him.

The only real solution for hate and anger is a heart transplant for all parties. Unfortunately, that isn't likely to happen anytime soon. But there's something you *can* do—role-model to your child positive ways to process and handle anger.

No parent expects their child to be the one on the evening news.

When the Unexpected Happens

In late 2014, 16 South Korean music fans died when they fell more than 65 feet at an outdoor K-pop concert due to the collapse of a ventilation grate.[4] Not one of those fans would have imagined that event would be their final farewell. But does that mean you should refuse to allow your 15-year-old son to accompany his friend and her parents to a concert he looks forward to in Los Angeles, just because something could happen at that big venue?

Life isn't safe. Accidents happen. A father of five is rear-ended on his way home from work, and his SUV is pushed into an oncoming truck on the expressway. A woman falls out of a golf cart and injures her brain. A bus full of children returning from a field trip overturns. None of these events are expected, yet they happen.

How you respond to such events tells your child everything about your life perspective and also shapes their worldview. Do they see from you an acceptance of those realities yet the drive to move on even when tragedies happen? Or do you sink into fear and what-ifs, controlled by negativity and paralyzed by the possibilities?

Personal Safety and Sexual Violence

Today's rape culture is, by its very design, the enemy of both men and women. That's why a dad I know insisted his 18-year-old daughter take a self-defense class before leaving for an urban college. He wanted her to learn as many techniques as possible to ensure her safety.

Gender violence (molestation, sexual assault, date rape, rape) doesn't have sex at its base as much as power and domination over someone. No one "asks for it." The act is a crime.

According to the Joyful Heart Foundation, "In the United States, one in three women and one in six men are survivors of sexual violence."[5] The crime affects people of all ages, sexual orientations, religions, genders, socioeconomic backgrounds, and education levels. That means neither your daughter nor your son is immune to becoming the target of such a criminal. So it's critically important you teach your children:

- To walk with purpose and confidence in public places. Sexual offenders are less likely to pick on competent-appearing children, because they are unable to dominate them as easily. At their core, sexual offenders are insecure, which is why they attempt to be powerful over others.

- Basic self-defense moves. That includes getting out of the grasp of someone grabbing you from behind. As one mother told her 12-year-old daughter, "If any person touches you inappropriately or grabs you and tries to get you to go with them, it's no-holds-barred. You bite, punch, and kick where it counts. I mean that. Don't worry about the other person."

- Commonsense tactics. If someone approaches you on the street, run for a building that has lights on and people inside. Yelling "Fire!" more easily gets a bystander's attention than commands like "Stop!" or "Help me!"

25

• When to fight and when to walk away . . . or run. With weapons so readily available and anger at its height in our nation, the ante is upped. Kids today no longer deal only with a bloody nose after fists on the playground. The stakes are deadly with handguns and knives.

Discrimination

Anyone who is "different" faces discrimination. It could be based on race, gender, special needs, adoption, or anything else that flags you as not the same as others in a group.

We've come a long way since 1951, when Oliver Brown tried to enroll Ruby, his African American daughter, into an all-white public school in Kansas. She was rejected simply because of her skin color.[6] Schools may have been desegregated back in the 1960s, but that doesn't mean racial tension has disappeared. Far from it. Events such as the shootings in Ferguson, Dallas, and Charleston, and angry standoffs between Chicago's police and the black community, show that prejudice remains a tragic issue for America.

But black-white prejudice isn't the only discrimination. In today's politically charged environment, those who don't speak English as their first language, are from Middle Eastern countries, or adopt specific religious traditions from their home country can be targets of hate crimes.

Children who are born with special needs or need additional assistance because of an accident or injury are treated differently from their "normal" peers. As Jamie said, "Why do people have to look at me that way? I'm just me."

Adopted kids face detractors who say they can't be loved as much by their parents because they aren't "biologically connected." Also, children whose ethnicity is different from their adoptive parents or who have parents of two distinct ethnicities often face prejudicial comments from classmates.

As Rhia told me, "I'm not black and I'm not white. Nobody knows how to treat me or what to say to me."

The same is true of LGBTQ youth. However, they often get hit harder because discrimination doesn't come only from outside sources; it also comes from their own families. No matter where you stand on the issue, it's one that can't be ignored.

When medical student Josh Eloge researched the causes of homelessness, he discovered a large number of the homeless population—an estimated 320,000 to 400,000 in the US—were LGBTQ youth. On average, they became homeless for the first time at age 14. Why? Because they ran away or were forced to leave when their families rejected them based on their sexual identity . . . even when many didn't disclose their sexual identity until *after* they became homeless. Because of the discrimination they face, these youth are much more likely to face substance abuse and mental health issues.[7]

No one, it seems, is safe from prejudice. Tests such as the IAT (Implicit Association Test), a long-term research project based at Harvard University, show that "very few of us are totally without prejudice of one form or another."[8] If you don't believe it, take the test yourself at www.implicit.harvard.edu.

As a parent, you want your child to be socially adept, understanding that not everyone is the same. But what do you do, for example, if you are in a predominantly Caucasian, upwardly mobile area and your kids aren't growing up with a lot of people of varying ethnic origins? Can you force them into accepting people who are different from them? No, you can't.

Instead, realizing that prejudice is a part of our world, bring up the topic with your kid around the dinner table. "I've been seeing a lot of news articles lately about the tension between *[name the issue]*. I'm wondering if you see any of that going on in your school or our neighborhood. If so, how do you handle it?" With such an approach, you can basically talk to your child about anything.

Or you could say, "Wow, it seems like kids are going out of their way to be unkind these days. I'm curious, because I don't go to school every day anymore, but you do—have you experienced any of that yourself?"

Anytime you say to a kid, "I'm curious what you think," you shower your child with respect. You're saying, "You matter in life, and in *my* life. What you think is important. What you feel is important. And guess what? It's okay to be different. We don't have to be all the same. There is great value in variety."

Yet, because of that variety, some people will be hateful, narrow-minded, and flagrantly disrespectful of others and their opinions.

> "It's okay to be different. We don't have to be all the same. There is great value in variety."

If you have a different view, you're slammed with a label you don't appreciate. Others take the view that everyone ought to do what they feel is right, and anything goes . . . as long as it's not murder. Still others don't want to judge, so they don't stand up for anything or anyone.

Where is the fine line?

You should draw lines in the sand for how to behave within your family and stick to those. If you don't stand for something, you won't amount to much. However, foisting those same personal guidelines on others is a dangerous and divisive game.

A year ago I talked to someone who was described to me as a strong man of faith. His daughter had left that faith in the dust when she left home, but she cared enough about her dad to show up at his house six months later with her surprise fiancé. Problem was, the fiancé was tatted up from head to toe, and the father didn't find that acceptable. Nor did he find the young man's language acceptable.

"So what did you do?" I asked the father.

He scowled. "I told him he wasn't welcome in my house looking like that and talking like that."

The rest of their conversation—or lack thereof—was what I'd expected.

The young man had used choice words to tell the father what to do with himself and left the house in a huff. What did the daughter do? She gave her dad the evil eye and followed her fiancé.

Father and daughter have been estranged ever since. Neither will give in. Because that father couldn't adjust his expectations and accept someone who was different, he lost his daughter and his son-in-law-to-be.

> If you don't stand for something, you won't amount to much. However, foisting those same personal guidelines on others is a dangerous and divisive game.

We all have biases. We don't like this or don't like that. Most of the time it's because we're uncomfortable, so we avoid "that type of person." But if we spend our time and energy checking off a list of things we don't like about that person, we'll never have a relationship with them. Just like that father.

When you rear kids, you have no idea who they will bring home to marry. You may think you know, but you don't. Accept whoever comes in the door with open arms. If you don't, you will shut out your daughter or son, who has chosen that person.

Does that mean you agree with everything that person does? No, but you choose not to look only at the outside. You take time to get to know the inside.

My mantra is, "It never hurts to be kind." Leave the judgment part up to Almighty God, where it belongs.

> My mantra is, "It never hurts to be kind." Leave the judgment part up to Almighty God, where it belongs.

Whoever your child brings home at any age—whether a friend or potential marriage partner—is their choice. To stay included in your child's life, you need to accept and welcome that person, even if doing so is out of your comfort zone.

Gangbangers

When I was a kid, I remember going to a park to play softball and getting kicked out by a neighborhood gang. I was told, "Hey, it's our turf. Get lost." That was years ago, and gangs are still staking their territory. Only now the stakes are higher.

Many of the deaths in Chicago—the current leading "Murder City" in our nation, surpassing New York City and Los Angeles— are gang related. They're retaliation murders from rival gangs or a result of territory warfare over drug sales.

If you and your family live in a small town, you're probably not worried about your child getting caught in the midst of gang crossfire. However, what happens when your teenager hops on the train to downtown Chicago, gets on the wrong EL on the way home, and ends up in gang territory? Such things do happen.

The better informed you and your child are, the calmer and more confident your child will be in any situation.

Take Carmen, a suburban 19-year-old who spent every Saturday for a year working solo with kids in Cabrini-Green, one of the poorest and most dangerous sections of Chicago. One look at her and you'd think that petite redhead could be blown over by a puff of wind. But she was empowered with knowledge that made her formidable—she knew that gangs existed because of a deep craving for acceptance. Everybody wants to be part of a group. If they don't get that in a positive way from family, they'll seek belonging elsewhere.

Her secret to win the kids' hearts? She started by bringing a backpack filled with treats and simple games. When she saw children playing in the dirt, she sat in the dirt near them and took out the treats and games. The children's curiosity won over their learned guardedness. Soon they gathered to eat, talk, and laugh. The next Saturday she was surrounded with those same children . . . and more.

Gradually she won the moms' respect by braiding hair, doing laundry, washing dishes, changing diapers—anything they were doing. No task was below her. She showed interest in learning how to cook their ethnic dishes.

Meanwhile, the men would linger back by the buildings, simply watching this white girl who didn't shrink back from their tough environment but accepted it as it was. Little by little, they began to interact with her in conversation.

One day four months later, it was already dark when she prepared to leave. Four young men approached her. "It's not safe to be here," one told her. They said something was about to go down with a rival gang and personally escorted her to the EL.

A young woman from the suburbs had won even gangbangers' hearts through the power of kindness.

Six years later, Carmen and her husband have continued her work in another area of Chicago-land with two different gangs.

> We are all fighting for the same thing—to be accepted for who we are and treated with respect, regardless of our situation in life.

Think for a second. That young woman could have spent her time being afraid of gang members. Instead, she realized that we are all fighting for the same thing—to be accepted for who we are and treated with respect, regardless of our situation in life. That truth empowered her to make connections that otherwise would have been impossible.

How do you respond to those who differ from you in background, social status, ethnicity, etc.? Do you accept them for who they are? Treat them with respect and a courteous attitude? Or do you hang back because they're different from you, and that makes them threatening?

Your child is watching you. How you respond in all situations becomes a model for how they will respond. So teach your kids how to be safe in uncertain environments. Teach them that not everyone has their best interests at heart, so they need to be careful. However, *you* be careful of categorizing people rather than considering them individually. Everyone wants to belong somewhere.

The "Whatever" Generation

You see on the news that there's a mass shooting in Orlando, Florida. The perpetrator shot five people and then killed himself. How do most of us respond?

We shake our heads and say, "Wow, what a crazy society."

Then, a minute later, we add, "Pass the potatoes."

We've been bombarded with so much violence in the news that most of us are anesthetized. That's particularly true of the majority of today's kids, who have grown up saturated with media stories of school shootings, gang violence, rape, terrorism, and war in places they've never been to. With instant access via the internet to anything happening in the world, they've read about so many of these tragic events that they're numb.

That's why they aren't likely to pay more than cursory attention to a terrorist attack in Israel. It's too far out of their everyday sphere. Yet they could tell you in a split second the title of the latest hit or what shenanigans their favorite artist is up to. They know what singers have fallen on stage or got caught driving drunk in the last month. They have earned professional degrees in Snapchat, Instagram, and Facebook.

However, very few have any idea of basic historical facts about their own country. For example, a late-night TV show host went out onto the streets of New York City and asked kids these simple questions:

- Who is the vice president of the United States?
- When did the United States become a country?
- Who was our first president?
- Who fought in the Civil War?
- What was the Revolutionary War about?

Most kids had no idea.

Parents continually worry about the broader issues—about their child's safety and how knowledge of what's going on in the world will impact their children emotionally. I know, because parents ask me about these issues as I travel around the country. They're concerned that terrorist attempts and school shootings will instill fear in their kids and damage their psyches.

The reality is, today's kids are too busy trying to stay alive in their own competitive sphere of peers to think about anything outside of it. Yes, they know what's going on—they're internet junkies, after all—but most of the time they aren't fearful or hurt by those issues, unless the issues become personal (see chapter 2).

The Exceptions—Sensitive Children

In some cases, with particularly sensitive children, knowledge of violent events outside their world can lead to uncertainty and fear.

One 7-year-old was traumatized by watching a *National Geographic* special about baby birds in Africa killed by a swarm of bees that invaded their nest. Her father, a nature enthusiast, had thought nothing about letting his daughter watch the special with him . . . until she woke up with a nightmare. It was her first brush with death, violence, and the reality that bad things happen on planet earth.

Parents of children who are exceptionally sensitive to visual input need to be cautious not only about what their children view on TV or in movies but also about putting a smartphone into their children's hands too early. Give them a cell phone where they can call you, but limit their internet access if possible. If a *National Geographic* special traumatizes her, what she can access on the internet in a click or two will do much more damage.

> **How much of life's harsh realities can your child handle? Only you can answer that question.**

You can't isolate your child from all the dangers and terrors of the world, nor should you. Bubble-wrapping your child will only harm her more when trouble hits personally, if she hasn't learned to grapple with the realities that bad things do indeed happen and life is not always fair.

Kids mature physically at different ages. They also mature psychologically at different ages. How much of life's harsh realities can your child handle? Only you can answer that question.

It all comes down to these questions: How well do you know your child? How will your child respond? Some children are greatly affected by outside stimuli.

Your 8-year-old sees footage of a shooting and gets a little scared. "Dad, what if that happened at my school? What would I do? Would I die?"

Now the parental roles you need to play are those of balancer and comforter. "That was a terrible thing. I saw it on TV this morning too. Sometimes bad things like that happen. But that kind of thing hasn't happened in our area. That school is 2,000 miles away. It would take us four days driving from morning to night to get there. We'd have to stay in a hotel three nights and eat breakfast somewhere else for four days just to reach that school."

Usually, by this time, a younger child will be sidetracked. You've answered his immediate question of, "What if that happened at

Cafe Special Offer

Valid from 2/1/20 through 2/29/20

FREE
Fresh Baked Cookie
with purchase of
any Grande or larger
Starbucks/Teavana
handcrafted beverage

To redeem: Present this coupon in the Cafe.

B7L3R4R

Customer choice of any flavor Fresh Baked
Cookie with qualifying beverage purchase.
This coupon may be redeemed only once per
customer. See Cafe cashier for details.

and audio books may not be returned, and can be exchanged only for the same product and only if defective. NOOKs purchased from other retailers or sellers are returnable only to the retailer or seller from which they were purchased pursuant to such retailer's or seller's return policy. Magazines, newspapers, eBooks, digital downloads, and used books are not returnable or exchangeable. Defective NOOKs may be exchanged at the store in accordance with the applicable warranty.

Returns or exchanges will not be permitted (i) after 30 days or without receipt or (ii) for product not carried by Barnes & Noble.com, (iii) for purchases made with a check less than 7 days prior to the date of return.

Policy on receipt may appear in two sections.

Return Policy

With a sales receipt or Barnes & Noble.com packing slip, a full refund in the original form of payment will be issued from any Barnes & Noble Booksellers store for returns of new and unread books, and unopened and undamaged music CDs, DVDs, vinyl records, electronics, toys/games and audio books made within 30 days of purchase from a Barnes & Noble Booksellers store or Barnes & Noble.com with the below exceptions:

Undamaged NOOKs purchased from any Barnes & Noble Booksellers store or from Barnes & Noble.com may be returned within 14 days when accompanied with a sales receipt or with a Barnes & Noble.com packing slip or may be exchanged within 30 days with a gift receipt.

A store credit for the purchase price will be issued (i) when a gift receipt is presented within 30 days of purchase, (ii) for all textbooks returns and exchanges, or (iii) when the original tender is PayPal.

Items purchased as part of a Buy One Get One or Buy Two, Get Third Free offer are available for exchange only, unless all items purchased as part of the offer are returned, in which case such items are available for a refund (in 30 days). Exchanges of the items sold at no cost are available only for items of equal or lesser value than the original cost of such item.

Opened music CDs, DVDs, vinyl records, electronics, toys/games, and audio books may not be returned, and can be exchanged only for the same product and only if defective. NOOKs purchased from other retailers or sellers are returnable only to the retailer or seller from which they were purchased pursuant to such retailer's or seller's return policy. Magazines, newspapers, eBooks, digital downloads, and used books are not returnable or exchangeable. Defective NOOKs may be exchanged at the store in accordance with the applicable warranty.

Returns or exchanges will not be permitted (i) after 30 days or my school?" His fear and uncertainty have dimmed because of your reassurance.

Younger children need you to minimize the news and reassure them that they are safe. In such a role you are the psychological blankie for your child.

If the question and fear come from your 15-year-old, you might say, "That was terrible, wasn't it? I can't imagine how devastated I'd be if that happened to you. I feel so bad for the families of the kids who died. They must be hurting terribly. But I'm also sad for the family of the kid who did the shooting. He must have been very angry at the world to do that. What do you think could make a kid so upset he'd want to hurt others?"

> **You are the psychological blankie for your child.**

Older children also need your reassurance, but they don't need you to minimize the news. They need a context in which to deal with the news.

You don't need to chase down every malady known to human-kind. Instead, you should answer the questions your child asks. When he is satisfied with the answer and has enough information, he'll stop asking. That's how you'll know how much to say and not say.

So take your cues from your child. If your daughter brings up a topic for the second or third time, you should pay attention to that smoke. Underneath it there's a high probability of a fire. Something is going on in her life that she is either wondering about or experiencing. She's testing the waters by seeing how you'll react to the initial topic.

For example, your daughter asks you about firearms, and you're startled. *Why is she asking me about guns? When was she ever interested in guns?*

Jumping on her for asking about the topic won't further your conversation. Instead, try, "Tell me more about that."

When she sees you're not freaking out at the question but are willing to gather more information, you'll find out she overheard two kids at school talking about getting even with a teacher. She's a little worried, since she likes that teacher.

Most kids aren't going to share easily with their parent what's going on in their lives. Their thoughts percolate.

Back when we used to brew coffee in percolator coffee makers, you'd first hear just a little pop. Then, when you heard a second pop, you knew the coffee was percolating. Within a short period of time, there would be a string of pops. Soon the aroma of fresh-brewed coffee would fill the air.

The same process happens with kids and thoughts. You have to wait patiently and listen for the pops. If there are multiples, a situation is brewing.

Children are naturally self-oriented. In order to grow empathy for those who are less fortunate and to become a contributing member of today's global society, they need to become aware of happenings in their own area and country and around the world.

No child can be truly grateful for what she has until she realizes that others live very differently. The most wonderful gift you can give your child is to grow her heart—to model and establish gratefulness as a daily occurrence in your home.

Practical Ways to Respond to "Out There" Issues

There's a fascinating movie called *Sully* about the American pilot Chesley Sullenberger, who became a hero after he landed his damaged plane on the Hudson River in order to save those on board. Even under extreme duress, he stayed focused and brought that airplane to rest safely.

When your child is hurting, that's the kind of role you need to play. Though you're under extreme duress in light of the circumstances and feeling your child's pain, you need to stay focused to help bring your family's plane to rest safely.

How can you respond practically to these larger world issues over which you have little or no control?

Give your child the gift of as much childhood as possible.

In the race to protect their kids against the evils of society, some parents overburden them with too much information. An example is stranger danger. Many parents overemphasize this danger, actually *creating* a fear in their children that wouldn't be there otherwise.

You certainly want your child to learn how to be careful because not everyone is kind, but your method of instruction shouldn't create fear that destroys innocence. If so, you end their childhood too soon—all of your own volition.

In the case of stranger danger, you don't need to say to a 5-year-old, "There are some very bad people who could hurt you, so you have to be careful. If anybody approaches you, then . . ."

Instead, keep it simple, especially with younger children. "Mommy or Daddy will always pick you up after school. If anyone tells you we sent them to get you, don't go with them. Run toward a teacher on the playground. Tell her what happened."

By saying something like that, you're introducing the possibility that an event like that might happen, so the child isn't surprised. Even more, you're preparing her with steps of what to do if that event does occur:

Step 1: Don't believe that person or get in the car.

Step 2: Go tell a teacher what happened.

Those steps keep the action plan simple, so your child is more likely to remember and not be fooled by a stranger.

With today's broken homes, though, it gets a bit more complicated. Some divorcing couples or exes use their children as pawns against each other. Sadly, many children who are reported as kidnapped are actually taken by family members, says the National Center for Missing & Exploited Children, which "intakes reports of missing children, including children who have been abducted, wrongfully retained or concealed by a parent or other family member."[9] If this is a situation you might find yourself in, knowing next steps up front would be extremely helpful to you.

You can also talk with the child's teacher and administration about any concerns you might have and provide paperwork to back up your statements. Note that this should be done with the adults at the school so that they are aware of any danger, but not with your child in the room.

If your child needs to know that he shouldn't go with Daddy, then if Daddy might try to pick him up from school, you can handle it with a simple comment like this: "Do you remember that Daddy sometimes got really angry and threw things? He needs time to work on that. So if he comes to pick you up at school, don't get in his car. Go back into the building and tell an adult in the office. They'll call me."

> As I always told my kids, "That little 'uh-oh' you hear inside is there for a reason."

Your child doesn't need to know all the ins and outs of your child support agreement. He just needs the basics to keep him safe. As he gets older, he'll learn more about his father's character, or lack thereof. Saying negative things about Daddy won't be helpful to either of you. Because he has been a part of your son's life, even a negative one, your son will feel his absence from your home.

In cases of separation or divorce, you walk a fine line between keeping childhood innocence intact and ensuring your child's safety in light of the grim realities of your daily battle with your ex or soon-to-be ex.

In facing the general ills of society, you can inoculate your child *and* teach basic street smarts without introducing fear. As I always told my kids, "That little 'uh-oh' you hear inside is there for a reason. It pops up to warn you that something is going on you should pay attention to. You shouldn't walk that direction, or you should avoid that potential conflict. Pay attention to that little voice."

Answer only the questions asked.

If a child asks you what time it is, you'd answer his question, right? You wouldn't develop an editorial position and expound for half an hour on how clocks are made, where they're manufactured, and all the types of facilities where they're sold, would you? You'd just tell him the time. That's all your child is asking. He only wants to know if he should put his shoes on so he's ready to get to his soccer match on schedule.

When children ask questions about bad things that happen to others in the world, you answer the question they ask, and no more. The answer you give must be age-appropriate and have as little additional information as possible. If your child wants to know more, he will ask. If that answer doesn't satisfy him, he'll ask more. It's best to err on the side of too little information than too much. Children are naturally curious. They'll push until they are satisfied. So don't jump on the full bandwagon too soon.

> It's best to err on the side of too little information than too much. Children are naturally curious. They'll push until they are satisfied.

Most parents think the topic of sex, for example, is a one-shot deal. You have "the talk" sometime in middle school, suffer through one uncomfortable big night of lecturing, and it's over.

Not so. The subject should be introduced a bit at a time as kids have questions. Seeing horses getting frisky at a local barn, the

---

Five Top To-Dos for Parents

- Tell the truth in love. Bad things happen to good people. It's a fact of life.
- Acknowledge that life isn't always fair or just.
- Balance your protective instinct with preparing your child for life on their own.
- Don't promote the victim mentality. It negatively shapes a child's worldview.
- Approach all life lessons as a learning experience.

---

announcement of a new baby in someone's family, or an awareness that boys and girls cover different body parts in swimsuits can kick off interesting discussions.

Again, answer only the questions your child asks, and no more, in age-appropriate lingo. When you do that, you're setting yourself up as the source of trusted information. Do that when they're age 5, and it's amazing what they'll feel comfortable asking you when they're 12, 13, 15, or even 17.

Nobody knows your child as well as you do. You can tell by his expression whether you've connected with him. If you answered his question honestly and provided the information he desires, he'll be satisfied. He'll walk away or switch to another subject.

Then you'll know you're through with that minor crisis . . . and ready for the next one.

Because there definitely will be a next one. It's a given in parenting.

Provide balance.

Let me assure you bluntly of one unchangeable fact. Just when you've weathered one storm in parenting, there will be another

40

one around the corner. Sometimes you'll be acting like an air traffic controller in the tower. Other days you'll be in the middle of the Running of the Bulls. Every parent wonders some days, *Holy crow, what's next?*

How you respond to each situation, though, is what's most important to your child's sense of stability and security. Why? Because you're the most important person in your child's life. You're their best role model of how to live life.

It's time to read your own barometer. What do you get anxious about in regard to your kids?

Violence is all around us. In the last 30 days, while I've been writing this book, there have been three incidents in England alone. You want your children to have a balanced approach to life—aware of the big dangers but not becoming incapacitated by or fearful of them—so how do you respond to the "out there" issues?

Be honest. "I saw that report too. There *are* people who are mean and want to hurt others, like the guy you saw on the news. But most are good people, helpful people. Like your teacher, Mrs. Jones, and Grandma and Grandpa. And remember when we got a flat tire last summer and Mommy didn't know what to do? A guy came along in a pickup and changed the tire."

Your child says, "Oh yeah, I remember that. We were on a road all by ourselves. It was so hot, and he was really nice."

So in that conversation, you've told your child that not all people are good and helpful, but most are. On one hand, he's seen the news report about the mean person. On the other hand, you've provided the balance by reminding him of the kind man who helped you out when you were stranded.

Solicit your child's thoughts and solutions.

One of the best conduits for conversations is the dinner table. Many families don't eat together because they're all running in separate directions. They catch food on the fly. But some of the Leman family's most stimulating conversations took place as we ate together.

When a big event such as a terrorist bombing happens, it's the smart parent who says to her 15-year-old, "Wow, it seems so crazy what's happening in the UK. I'm sure you saw it too. Another bombing. And this time . . . *[give a few details to show you paid attention]*. I'm still struggling with how I feel about that. Why would somebody do that? Frankly, I don't have any answers. I'd love to know what you think. Sometimes things that happen like that seem so far away, like an unreal movie. Other times they scare the pants off me, wondering what if it happened in our town."

Anytime you tell a child, "I'd love to know what you think" or "I'm curious about what you think," you are treating her as a social equal. You're inviting conversation and creating a relationship where your daughter can talk to you about anything, even things not easy to discuss.

That's how you solicit conversation from your teenager. Difficult issues and horrific events surround us every day. But getting your child to talk about them, well, that's another matter.

If you want your child to keep talking to you, toss out a topic and see if she bites on it. If so, open the conversation. If not, let it go. You'll have another opportunity soon.

Often the best way to get your older child to talk is for you to shut up and listen.

Create an environment of safety.

Your child's world is really quite small. It's his house or apartment, parent(s), siblings, grandma and grandpa, and the family dog. He has his preschool, kindergarten, or elementary school. He doesn't go far—maybe to the grocery store or to the park to play. He needs to know and feel safe in that defined world.

You, parent, are the only one who can create that environment of safety. So when your toddler falls, what do you do? You kiss his boo-boo, and life is instantly better. You become the parent who can solve anything.

As your child grows older, more people enter his world. It becomes larger. More questions surface and more issues are introduced. But home remains a secure environment. Home is the place with unconditional love and a predictable routine.

In middle school and high school, students do become aware of more "out there" things. There will be times when those bigger global issues will intersect with your child and hurt her. That's when she will ask, "Why did this happen to me?" She will experience frustration, fear, and anger. She won't have the longer-life perspective that adults have to know that bad things do indeed happen to good people.

But you remain calm. You know two very important things:

1. No one is immune to the power of these overarching big issues. They were going to hit sometime. It's best for them to happen in her world when you're there to walk alongside her.

2. It isn't the issues themselves but your child's *responses* to them that will help shape her character and direct her next moves.

You're not helpless. You don't have to be a bench sitter, watching life go by. You can choose to step up to the plate and be the parent you need to be for your child's sake. That means you'll make tough decisions. You'll say no when you need to. You'll encourage your child. You'll be her advocate.

As my daughter Hannah—communications director for Children's HopeChest, a global orphan-care organization—says, "We believe that life isn't always black and white, and that in the gray and the messiness of life is where transformation happens and life is truly lived out."[10]

Every child longs for a hero. The best hero of all is you, because you aren't afraid of that messiness. Because you love your child unconditionally, you simply roll up your sleeves and plunge in.

You can't control what is "out there," but you can control what happens inside your home. So be the champion she needs you to be.

2

When Hurt Hits Home

Issues don't truly become personal until they are personal.

I'll never forget my wife laboring to birth our firstborn. As she struggled in pain, I tried my husbandly best to comfort her. "It's okay, honey. Everything will be okay," I kept assuring her.

Finally, my kind, sweet-spoken wife, who can't even swat a fly, looked up at me. "Well," she growled, "everything might be okay up there, but it's *not* okay down here."

That's when I truly realized that a baby is bigger than the birth canal.

At the time I wore a University of Arizona grad ring that I was very proud of, since I didn't think I could ever get into the school, much less graduate. Even after our baby was born I could still see the indentation on my pinky, close to the ring finger, because Sande had squeezed my hand so hard.

That day was a good reminder that issues don't become personal until they *are* personal.

In this chapter, I'll give you an overview of three basic categories of hurts that hit home—Family, Self, and Peers—and some principles for how you can better understand and assist your child. For even more specifics on these issues, you'll find the "Ask Dr. Leman" section helpful.

Family

It's true that those you love the most and count on the most can also hurt you the most. That's because the relationship you have with them is much closer and deeper. This is particularly true in the arena of family. Divorce, custody battles, and MIA parenting cause significant rifts in families, leading to insecurity, anger, and hurt. Questions about adoption ("Why did my birth parents give me away?"), loss ("Why did my sister have to die?"), and abuse ("Was what happened my fault?") drive wedges further into kids' hearts.

Understanding what your child really thinks and feels about these events and others will help you act proactively and in your child's best interests as you navigate the situation together.

Divorce

One of the biggest reasons kids hurt today is because of the disintegration of families through divorce. Children have real questions that need to be answered:

"Why did this happen to me? Why was it *my* family that had to fall apart?"

"If my parents don't love each other, will they no longer love me?"

"If my dad leaves my mom, will I not see him anymore? Then what if my mom leaves me too?"

"Is it my fault? Did I cause them to split up? Do they hate me?"

"What if my mom doesn't have enough money to keep our house? Will we have to move? Will I have to change schools? What about my younger brother?"

"Will Mom and Dad split up us kids? Sometimes I don't like my sister, but I still want to live with her."

Many children of divorce worry about their parents now that they're solo. They fantasize that their parents will get back together and everything will be wonderful. That's a pipe dream usually quite far from reality. There's a reason that you and your spouse are divorcing.

When I get a room of kids from divorcing or divorced homes together, I ask the question, "If things could be different, would you want your mom and dad back together?"

A few kids have told me they're glad their parents separated, since they were fighting all the time. Living apart relieved so much of the constant tension. But the majority of them say yes. Why would they want that, especially if you two fought all the time? Because the mundane, the predictable, the routine is what gives kids security. Long story short, they'd rather you still be together in the same house and fighting like cats and dogs than living in two separate houses. If you live separately, they are torn between the two of you. *Where do I go for Christmas and Easter? Mom's or Dad's? What if they're offended if I choose to go to the other parent's house?*

Some kids will create their own fantasy stories about the parent who has left, making them a better human being than you'd ever give them credit for. Other kids see the loneliness of the parent they're living with and hatch matchmaking schemes, targeting a neighbor or coach as a potential new spouse for their parent.

To understand how kids facing divorce feel, think of them as the dried-out turkey wishbone after Thanksgiving. They've got Mom pulling on one end and Dad pulling on the other, and they're feeling the pain of being stretched both directions. Their parents are fighting, and there are rumors of divorce. When the two sides of the wishbone become too brittle, they break. Then life becomes surreal for the kids, who are defenseless against the changes. One parent is moving out of the house, or the kids are moving out with one of the parents.

What do most parents do? They go into what I call the "not your fault" frenzy. "It's not your fault. This is between us," they tell their kids. "It has nothing to do with you."

Nothing to do with the kids? It has *everything* to do with them. It tears their life apart as they know it.

Parents who are divorcing are under all kinds of stress—emotional, financial, and physical. As one woman told me recently, "I was completely blindsided. That's what hurts the most. I never saw it coming." She felt like she'd been slapped in the face by her husband's adultery, and she was free-falling down the hill of self-worth. Her husband had already moved into an apartment with his girlfriend. She was left to explain to her young kids what had happened to their daddy.

> To understand how kids facing divorce feel, think of them as the dried-out turkey wishbone after Thanksgiving. They've got Mom pulling on one end and Dad pulling on the other.

How exactly do you explain divorce to a child? The loss of trust and betrayal can lead to questions about what love really is, which can deeply affect a child's future relationships.

There's no such thing as an easy divorce. It's not easy for anyone. Yet if you walk into a card store, I bet you could find at least one card that says, "Congrats on your divorce." Even though divorce is prevalent, it's a sucker punch for any kid.

Don't be fooled by your kids if they look like they're cruising through your divorce. They're not. None of you are.

Some of you are freaking out right now. "Hey, wait a minute," you're saying. "I'm so glad I divorced. I got away from one of the biggest all-time losers on this earth."

There's a reason you're relieved. But that doesn't mean your child is.

How Kids Respond

Every child in your family will grapple with the hurt of divorce in a different way. Here are a few of the common defense mechanisms kids use to protect themselves.

Kid #1: He will shrug and say, "Hey, it's no big deal. It doesn't bother me. It's better than them fighting." What he means, though, is the opposite. His world is being ripped apart. The only way he can deal with all the upheaval is to act like it doesn't matter. But it matters deeply. Such a child is giving you the straight arm so you keep your distance. He's working hard to avoid any conflict because he's afraid he'll fall apart. He doesn't want to rock the boat and wants everyone to get along as much as possible. *If I just lay low, maybe this will all blow over*, he thinks.

I assure you, though, that kid is lying awake at night thinking about the divorce, and it bothers the heck out of him. He's probably silently crying himself to sleep.

> **Just like every parent wants a happy kid, every kid wants a happy parent.**

Kid #2: She becomes the adult when she sees the fragility of her parents (particularly Mom). So she tries to calm the ruffled waters. Just like every parent wants a happy kid, every kid wants a happy parent. In both cases, it's an unreal expectation. We're not always happy in life. Yet this kid works hard to give equal time to each parent. For example, even though she's more comfortable living with Mom, she goes out of her way to spend time with Dad because she doesn't want him to feel left out.

It's even more difficult and complicated for kids to navigate this new world if their mom or dad has a new friend. They've always seen you, Mom and Dad, as a couple, but now there's this *thing* living with their dad. Imagine what their first response is when they meet the *thing*. It isn't pretty or comfortable for anyone.

The majority of these kids feel forced to take a side between Mom and Dad. Then there's a war of words and more disruption in the family. Very few kids can face their parents' divorce by saying pragmatically, "Hey, divorce is a sign of our times. I'm like a lot of other kids. So I might as well suck it up and get through this."

Kid #3: This kid will hide out. She'll get quiet and conceal her feelings. But let me assure you, still waters do run deep, and they can be incredibly dangerous. She's likely sticking her head in the sand emotionally and isolating herself so she can ask herself terrifying questions such as, "What's going to happen to me? What if Mom leaves too?" Someday her passionate internal nature will come out and shock everyone with its intensity.

Kid #4: This kid gets outwardly angry to handle his inward pain. He strikes out at everyone around him—sister, brother, parents, the world. He may purposefully do things like destroy a sibling's toy, leave his bike out in the rain, or ruin his dad's prize baseball card to get attention.

What is this surly, antagonistic kid saying when he argues about everything? "I feel hurt by life. Therefore, I have the right to strike out at others and to make them miserable."

Kid #5: She becomes the drama queen who overreacts to everything:

"How come things aren't like they were?"

"Why do we have to do this? It's stupid."

"Can't we just do it like we used to?"

Her attention is so focused on her own emotionally messy state that she doesn't show much understanding of the new financial situation or any new restrictions. She acts clueless because she is. But underneath her behavior is a boatload of hurt.

Custody Battles

The essential question at the core of custody battles is, "Who is going to win here?" It's an extension of the pull and push between the parents that caused the divorce in the first place. In the middle between the warring parties are the children. The truth is that it's often out of vindictiveness that someone insists on custody.

Joy was in just such a situation, with her soon-to-be ex trying to get back at her by filing for full custody of the kids. She was shocked when I advised her, "Look him right in the eye and say, 'Okay, you can have the kids.'"

> The essential question at the core of custody battles is, "Who is going to win here?"

But her backing off did the trick. The husband was the CEO of a company. What was he going to do with three kids under the age of seven at home? Take them to his mother's house three states away?

So if your ex unrealistically wants the kids, don't fight. Take the "you want 'em, you take 'em" approach. You'll save yourself a boatload in legal fees and still end up with the kids. Even if he takes them initially, chances are by the end of a couple of weeks, when he's used up his vacation time and can't find anyone to watch them, he'll decide that you would be a better custodian.

The Best Ways to Help Your Kids

When you're hurting yourself from this turn of events in your life, what can you do for your kids?

1. Be the adult. Don't bring your personal business and squabbles into your conversation with your kids. Don't use them as your sounding board for all the things you hate about your ex. If you start putting down your ex in front of your

kids, you're only asking for them to defend him vociferously. It's far better to extend that olive branch to your ex-spouse, even if he doesn't deserve it, for the kids' sake. Getting into a power struggle won't help any of you. The ones who pay for it the most are your kids.

2. Don't hammer your kids with questions. Specifically, don't ask what they do when they are with your ex. You aren't licensed to be a private eye, so don't go there. Instead, ask your children about their thoughts and feelings. "I know this is tough on everybody. I want to know how you're doing. You okay?" Turn the focus to them and their activities rather than on the difficulties of your divorce.

3. Make as few changes as possible during this tumultuous time. The very nature of divorce creates all kinds of changes—moving apartments, selling a home, moving to a different school district. But keep things as simple and close to what your child is used to as you can.

4. Don't bounce your kid around like a rubber ball. With most divorces, parents want to split the kid in half and do the 50/50 thing. I'm adamantly against that approach because of the toll it takes on the kids, who are already stressed. I always tell divorcing couples, "If you're so high on having to spend equal time with your kid, then you two move from place to place and let the kid stay in his own home."

Now I know that sounds improbable and even a little crazy—especially when you can't agree on anything and that's why you got divorced—but consider this. Your kids are young. Many of them still believe a guy in a red outfit who drives reindeer comes down the chimney every Christmas. Even older kids are more innocent and gullible than you think.

You are the adults. Your kids are kids. Each of you should act in your respective roles.

5. Realize that your kids need time with their friends. Those friends are their lifeline to sanity and normalcy when their world as they know it is being turned upside down. If your divorce includes moving out of your neighborhood, go out of your way to keep your child connected to his old friends. Maybe now you live in a two-bedroom apartment instead of a two-floor house. You can still stuff that apartment with kids, buy some pizza, and let them have some fun. They won't care if the environment isn't as posh as it used to be. All they care is that there's food and acceptance there.

6. Allow your kids to be a little uneven emotionally. Divorce has just dropped a psychological bomb in your child's life, so he'll be understandably upset. If he's part of the hormone group, he's already whacked out. That means he needs grace from you when he's not perfect. However—and this is the really tough part as a parent—you cannot let guilt run your life. If you do, you will excuse behaviors that you never should, such as disrespect and foul language.

> **You are the adults. Your kids are kids. Each of you should act in your respective roles.**

Giving your child some leeway to express himself doesn't mean you accept the unacceptable, which includes any put-downs. You are now the head of your family, and your child has to respect you. Accept that there will be blowups. But those are never an excuse for running over you. You may not take the problem on in the heat of the moment for whatever reason, but the next day, when things are calmer, is fair game.

"I want to circle back to what happened yesterday and tell you that what you said really hurt. I know that you're hurting. I am too. But I am not your psychological punching bag. I'm your mother. Yes, this is tough for both of us. We *will* get through it, but I want to do so in a healthy manner. I will do my part the best I can, and I need you to do your part the best you can too. Can we agree on that?"

7. Have a game plan. In these uncertain times, previous traditions have been thrown up in the air. Maybe Saturday morning was always daddy/daughter time or Friday night was girls' night. In the absence of those relationships, make a game plan that you can post on the fridge. It can be weekly, monthly, or long-term. Schedule activities and deadlines.

The important thing is that the schedule shows onward movement. Your family isn't stuck because of this event. Someone is in charge, still leading the flock. You are that decisive leader. You need to be supportive, understanding, and positive and take action.

If you do these things, you provide a stable environment for your kids.

Six Traits of a Healthy Home

- Hurts are acknowledged and addressed, not ignored.
- All members are held accountable, respect each other, and contribute to the family.
- The truth is told in love and not minimized.
- The values of courage, perseverance, responsibility, self-discipline, kindness, compassion, shared beliefs, honesty, loyalty, and a strong work ethic are an unshakable foundation.
- Problems are proactively and kindly addressed with creative solutions that fit the situation.
- Unconditional love and support reign.

MIA Parent

Parents can be missing in action for any reason. Perhaps you never married the father of your child, or he has shown little interest in your kid since the divorce. Or that man still lives in your house but he's emotionally absent. He might still bring home some of the bacon, but he's not really there for you and the kids. You often feel like it's you and your kids against the world.

The Ex

You found yourself an instant single parent through a situation not of your making or choosing. Now you've moved from Seattle, Washington, to Little Rock, Arkansas, because that's where your mom, dad, and older sister live. You needed emotional support and financial help to raise your two kids after your husband divorced you.

> Grant in fantasy what you can't in reality.

A month after your move to Arkansas, your 9-year-old son says, "I miss Daddy."

Verbalizing what you really think about that man won't help either of you. So you grant in fantasy what you can't in reality.

"I bet you do," you tell him. "And I'm sure he misses you."

"I want to go see Dad tomorrow," he says.

You know that's impossible. A plane ticket to Seattle isn't in your budget. But you say, "Wouldn't that be great to just hop on an airplane and do that?"

Dream a bit with your son. Then bring him gently back to reality. "I wish that could happen, but we don't have the money to hop on a plane. And anyway, you have a game this weekend."

It's a fine balancing act—an art form, in fact—to pull this off positively. But I know you can do it, because that's how deeply you care about your child.

The Abdicator

As I travel around the country, women tell me about this common scenario.

"He buries himself in work and is rarely there for me and the kids. When I talk to him about it, he gets angry and says, 'Well, who do you think I'm doing all this for? You and the kids.' How can I get him to pay some attention to us? I can't stand to see the hurt in my daughter's eyes when her daddy doesn't show. If he does, belatedly, she climbs all over him. Since he only sees her when she's happy, he doesn't know how upset she was. I'm the one who has to deal with the emotional fallout. He just doesn't get that it's important for him to show up, on time. Sometimes I get really angry."

Of course you do, Velcro mom, because you are basically doing everything in a two-parent home. This isn't what you signed up for. Your partner has abdicated his role as a parent. Perhaps he sees it as "women's work," or he's single-mindedly thinking about his career track and assumes, *I've got the family job done. They're doing all right.*

Add to that the fact that many of you also work outside the home and juggle your own career too. During your precious half-hour lunch break, you manage a granola bar in between making your kid's dentist appointment, scheduling your pet for a nail trim, and researching the remainder of the work project that's due in an hour. Then you get a text from your husband, asking you to pick up a cheese-and-cracker tray on your way home since he needs it for a work event the next day.

No wonder you're feeling a little tired and testy by the time you see that man of yours by evening. And what does he do? Puts his feet up after dinner and does a TV brain rinse while you stare at the mountains of dishes that somehow accumulated all by themselves.

Everything indeed does stick to you like Velcro. And if you're like most women, you can't just let those projects go. You're the one still doing those dishes at 1:00 a.m.

That's why, whenever I talk to fathers, I say bluntly, "If you're there for the launching, you ought to be there for the rest of it too."

> "If you're there for the launching, you ought to be there for the rest of it too."

It's a smart man who learns how to grocery shop, cook, and leave his busy accountant job an hour early to be at his son's Little League game. No woman can be without a relief pitcher as a parent.

That goes for men too. Some stay-at-home dads are in this same situation with their on-the-go wives.

If your spouse has abdicated their role, it's time for a discussion.

"I don't think you mean to do this, but you're really hurting your son. Every time he walks out onto the field, I see him looking up in the stands to see if you're there. He's so disappointed when you're not. You've asked me to tape his games so many times, and like a robot, I do that. But I'm done. I'm not doing it anymore. You need to come and see the game for yourself. If you want to record it yourself, that's great."

You have to take a stand. It's my two-by-four theory. Sometimes a woman has to take a two-by-four and whack her husband on the side of the head. With some men, it's the only way they'll respond if there's a crisis. So if you have to start the crisis with a bit of drama-queen behavior (your teenage daughter can show you just how it should be done), then do it.

The years when those kids are in your nest will fly by. You don't want your husband to miss out.

The other factor is that if you're giving, giving, and giving more and not getting anything back or getting any support for the kids, you'll become starved emotionally. You don't need a shrink to tell you where your marriage is heading.

So don't let the sun go down before you have this conversation. It's too important to let this go. Yes, your guy may be concerned about his company downsizing. He may be acting this way because he's fearful that if he doesn't continue to give 150 percent at work, he'll find himself on the short list. However, if he doesn't pay attention to his family, he won't have anyone to come home to.

The biggest question is, What's more important—your kids or things?

I trust you'll say your kids. The reward of their smiles will be priceless.

Adoption

There's no way to adequately describe the joy I felt when I saw my daughter Hannah with her newly adopted twins. It was pure bliss. Those two babies are the apples of their grandpa's eye, along with my two other grandkids. In my view all children are God's children, and there is no difference. However, as adopted children grow, they will encounter significant questions. Depending on the age and personality of your child, some will struggle greatly as they search for the answers.

Every adoption starts with a loss. With international adoption, rarely do you have any information about the birth parents. With domestic adoption, you can usually find out some details about the birth parents and get basic medical history. However, every adopted child has a history of some kind. Some were adopted as babies, others as toddlers, and some not until their school years. Especially in adolescent years, as they discover they look different and act different from their adoptive families, they will ask:

"Why did my birth mom and dad give me up? Why didn't they keep me?"

"If I found them, would they take me back?"

"If they gave me up, will Mom and Dad give me up if I'm not good?"

"Didn't they love me?"

"Was I not worth it?"

"Do Mom and Dad love me as much as their 'real' (biological) kids?"

These are just a few of the large questions that face adopted children. Pieces of their life are missing, and they will feel that void no matter how much you love them and accept them.

What can you do?

1. Talk about the adoption. Adopted kids don't always have birth stories (though in a few special cases, you might have been in the room for a domestic birth), so tell how you felt when you heard about their existence. Use details. Describe the joy, the longing, and how you waited with anticipation for them to join your family.

2. Celebrate the day the child arrived in your family. Tell the story of that event over and over. A family I know who adopted internationally calls it "Gotcha Day" and celebrates it with a special event and a gift from their child's home country every year. To that child, Gotcha Day is more important than her own birthday since pictures of the day she joined their family abound, whereas she has no pictures of her birth.

3. If your child is a different ethnicity, explore that heritage with him. Help him to learn the language so it is easier for him to navigate that culture as an adult as well. Every day he walks the fine line between two ethnicities, whether he realizes it now or not. Understanding both cultures will assist him greatly both now and in the future.

4. Realize that because there is some history with your adopted child, she may face issues your other kids don't have. Adopted children often struggle with fears of abandonment, betrayal, and being left alone. They may have low self-worth, thinking something is wrong with them because their birth parents "gave them up." They may also fear changing their environment. These are not just imagined issues but real ones based on their background experiences.

> Adopted children often struggle with fears of abandonment, betrayal, and being left alone.

Many adoptive parents initially think, *Well, if I just love her enough, that issue will go away.* You can't love those intense feelings and memories out of existence. But if you understand them and explain to your child why she feels that way sometimes, you've paved the way to psychological health.

When those feelings crop up in the difficult teen years, she can think, *Wow, I'm really scared right now. I didn't expect Dad to go away on that long trip. But I know why I'm scared. I'm afraid he won't come back, like my birth mom and dad didn't. They left me. But Dad isn't going to leave me. He'll come back when his business is done.*

Because you've helped her identify why she feels fearful sometimes, she can often reason herself out of the panic she feels. You've given her the tools to forge on to a healthy adulthood.

5. Be the balancer. Even the best-adjusted adopted kids still feel the sting of rejection. For them to be in your family, someone did have to "give them away" (as much as adoptive parents and adoption agencies dislike that term). They are a wonderful gift to you, but leaving their birth parents is a

part of the package deal. When your adopted child is feeling insecure, emphasize that he was the most fabulous gift you have ever received. But also acknowledge his hurt.

"I know you will always wonder about your birth parents. Where are they? What happened to them? Why did they decide to place you for adoption? Why didn't they want you? You can talk to me about those questions anytime. I'll do what I can to help you find the answers, if we can, when you're ready."

Many parents of adopted children don't want to address those questions openly for fear their kids will feel more hurt, or that talking about the questions will serve only as a reminder that the kid is "different." But let me assure you, your kid is thinking about those questions anyway. It's much better to get them out in the open.

Secrets shared are less burdensome, and they draw you closer together.

Loss through Illness or Death

I can't count the number of doctors I know or have read about who chose their vocation because a parent or sibling died of a certain disease. Watching a loved one suffer and die has a deep psychological impact on a child. It can also trigger fears that other family members will get sick and die.

Justin watched as his little sister lost her hair and then the ability to walk due to cancer. Several years later, her body was too tired to fight, and she passed away. Fast forward a year, when his mom got the flu and had to stay in bed for a few days. Justin blurted out, "Mommy, are you going to die too?"

Truth is, people get ill. You can try to live a healthy lifestyle—exercising, eating right—but illness happens. Everyone is born and everyone dies.

Is it sad? Yes, but dying is a part of the life cycle, just like when leaves wither and fall from trees every autumn. That's the honest answer.

How can you help in times of loss?

1. Have real, honest conversations. Instead of saying to a child, "God took your sister away. He knew she'd be happier and not in pain if she was in heaven," it would be far better to say, "I miss your sister too. I don't understand why she had to leave us, especially so soon. I wish we could have had her with us longer. Do you remember when . . . *[share some memory you have of her]*?" Such a response keeps communication doors open.

   Asking why is an honest question, and it should never be shut down. Sometimes there are no answers, and you can't drum them up, as much as you try. Getting angry about life being unjust is honest too. You can't control everything that happens to those you love, but you can be honest about not having all the answers.

   > **Asking why is an honest question, and it should never be shut down.**

   Allow your child the space to be real, and follow the same rule yourself. Then both of you can get through this tragedy and emerge stronger together.

2. Never be afraid of tears. They're healthy and healing. Your child will be comforted just by knowing you care. We can't control everything that happens to us and those we love. Crying is a necessary release valve.

3. Talk about their fears.

   Becca was on the phone with a girlfriend, laughing about finding her first gray hair. An instant later, she heard a glass shatter as it fell to the floor behind her. Her daughter, an only child, had dropped her orange juice glass. Mandy raced toward her mother and hugged her legs, refusing to let go. "Are you going to die like Grandma? Please tell me you won't, Mommy!"

Becca was astounded. Her 5-year-old daughter somehow thought that since Grandma, who had passed away recently, had gray hair, then having graying hair meant you were going to die.

Some of the connections children make are disturbing and unnerving. Nevertheless, they think them. Isn't it better that they know they can talk about their fears—real and imagined—with you, the one they trust the most?

4. Be proactive. When something bad happens to someone you love, be proactive when you hear the news. Communicate to the person your thoughts, feelings, and love for them. Bring flowers. Children can make a card and go with you to visit the ill person.

Communicate that not everyone who has an illness is going to die. "Uncle Phil is going through a hard time right now," you tell your child. "What he needs most is to know that people care for him, are thinking of him, and are praying for him. He needs our love. What do you think we could do to show him that?"

Engage your child in the search for a solution. One little boy took his model cars, tied them together bumper to bumper, and strung them across his older brother's hospital room. Why? Because the two boys had always played with the model cars together. Chris wanted his brother Chase to know that even when he was in school and couldn't be at the hospital, he was thinking of him.

Kids are wonderfully creative. Allow them to be a part of the solution.

5. Keep the loved one alive in your memory. Talk openly about experiences you had with the person who has passed away.

Laugh, shed tears, and process together. Just because that person is no longer on this earth doesn't mean their influence and life lessons have to stop.

Abuse

There is nothing worse than being abused by someone you trust, or having it happen in a place that you consider safe and where you spend the majority of your time. It is the most horrific of all betrayals to a child and has a lasting impact on his worldview and relationships.

In today's fragmented world, with complicated family relationships, abuse is on the rise. Abuse can be verbal, physical, emotional, or sexual. Abuse is not a mistake, a one-time happening because someone got angry or had extra testosterone coursing through their veins that made them act in such a way. No, abuse is a crime.

Sexual abuse is the huge elephant on the couch that no one wants to talk about. One in four women are sexually assaulted on college campuses, for example.[1] Sadly, there's a higher probability that sexual abuse will happen in a child's home than anywhere else. It can also come from extended family members or trusted individuals your child has a lot of interaction with—her swim coach, his Little League coach, a babysitter, the next-door neighbor.

With sexual abuse, people mistakenly assume it's all about the sex. But it's more about the wielding of power over someone weaker. Neither boys nor girls are immune. Though there are more male abusers (fathers, stepfathers, uncles, brothers, cousins), females can also be abusers. The females are less likely to be reported, though, because of the cultural shame factor boys feel at being dominated by women. Also, don't assume sexual abuse is all male to female or female to male. It can be female to female or male to male.

Kids who are being abused will often keep that knowledge a secret, due to shame that it's their fault, the resulting low self-worth, or fear. Abusers often hold two cards over a child's head: "If you don't do what I say, I'll kill you," or, "If you don't do what I say, I'll do this to your sister." As a result, the child harbors her fear inside and takes the hits silently unless someone steps in to help her.

You, parent, have to be her protector, even if that means going against your spouse, your live-in, your brother, or even one of your other children. Jen, a working mom, was devastated when she found out her older son was sexually abusing her 7-year-old daughter after bringing her home from school.

The unexpected can happen . . . right in your own home. If you see any hint of abuse, get to the bottom of it immediately.

Oprah Winfrey got straight As on her report card as a child. She was kind, giving to others, and outwardly compliant. Yet she experienced childhood abuse firsthand. She was brutally raped at age 9, then faced "constant episodes of sexual molestation between the ages of 10 and 14, as well as a series of physical abuse," she reported in an interview with David Letterman nearly five decades after the events occurred.[2]

Clearly these events had a powerful influence on her life. Yet Oprah made a choice to turn that horrific experience into a life path of inspiring others.

"Anybody who has been verbally abused or physically abused will spend a great deal of their life building their self-esteem," she said. "Everyone is looking for that validation. I know what it feels like to not be wanted. . . . You can use it as a stepping stone to build great empathy for people."[3]

If your child is being abused in any way, or if you even suspect something might be going on, take these steps:

1. Everything else in your life has to stop. You should investigate immediately.

2. Ask your child gently about any experiences. Most importantly, believe what your child says.

3. Separate the child and the abuser immediately. Don't leave them alone together for any reason.

4. If the abuse has happened in your own home, go with your child to a safe place.

5. Report the abuse to the police. Have them help you with next steps legally. Pursue the abuser to the full extent of the law. Even if they are a family member, you owe that to your child . . . and any other children the abuser may come in contact with. Because of the abuse, your family relationships are already severely fractured. You can't make anything worse than it already is by taking action. Your child, who has been violated, needs to feel your love and support. She needs you to be an immovable rock when it comes to drawing the line about right and wrong legally.

6. Get involved with an abuse recovery group. (There are also groups for rape recovery.) I recommend counseling one-on-one as well. Children who suffer abuse may need additional counseling as they mature and ask deeper questions about their childhood experience.

Every child who has been abused feels secret shame. *It must be my fault*, she thinks, *or he wouldn't treat me that way.* Self-doubt, humiliation, and guilt abound. Your child needs to know:

- She did nothing to deserve this. It is not her fault.
- A crime was committed against her, and that criminal will have to pay for what he did wrong.
- You love her, believe her, and support her. You will do whatever you can to help.
- She is safe in her home now with you. No one will get to her.
- You believe she's strong and will get through this.

∞

In any family issue, you are the emotional barometer for your child. The hurts of life will come, but they don't have to crush you or your child.

Your child will take his cues from you. When he's hurting, he'll model his responses after the way you respond. If you don't overreact when faced with divorce, custody battles, the questions of adopted kids, and loss, your kids won't either. So take family hardships in stride as part of living on planet earth. Show compassion, love, and concern to your kids. Walk alongside them as they realize that we all die at some time. Allow them to process and cry without judgment.

And remember, if abuse is going on in your home, it needs to stop right now. Your child needs and deserves her home to be a safe place.

Will your road ahead be difficult? Yes. But you can rise above this together.

Self

Children undergo tremendous changes as they are growing—bodies, hormones, relationships, living situations, etc. It's no wonder they feel a great deal of emotional stress at times.

If you grew three inches in one summer, got your period, and heard the guy you like really likes someone else, you'd be stressed.

If you had your first wet dream, you became suddenly aware of these wonderful creatures called females, and your voice cracked as you were talking to the most popular girl in school, you'd be stressed.

Now add sibling squabbles and overhearing your parents fight about money to that mix. Throw in trying to keep your competitive edge with your peers. That would be a boatload of stress, wouldn't it?

Such stress, if left unchecked, can pile up and lead to depression, eating disorders, cutting, and suicide attempts, to name a few top concerns of parents.

One of the greatest mistakes parents make is assuming that all is "fine" in their kids' lives if they aren't "acting up." Your child may look like she is coping well with life on her own. But because every child craves the understanding, support, and unconditional love of her parents, she's doing her best to hide her imperfections from you. She'll do so especially if you tend to criticize things she does or point out how she can do something better.

Because "self" issues are internal, what symptoms do you look for to know if your child is in trouble?

Depression

Parents ask me all the time, "My kid seems really down. How do I know if this is only a phase or she's really depressed and needs help?"

I'm never one to immediately recommend that you run to your neighborhood shrink if you think your child is acting depressed. That's because some children are easily stressed. When things don't go perfectly, they fall apart. They cry because they're upset. Or they withdraw to their bedroom for an evening or a day. Part of their behavior is purposeful so that you will know life is not working out for them and feel sorry for them. They want you to feel their pain.

If you overplay your cards with these kids, they will work you as a parent. They know where your buttons are.

Let's say your daughter had a terrible day because she was betrayed by her friend group. She's crying when she walks in the door and refuses to come out for dinner. She won't even eat the special dessert you made because you knew she was feeling low.

What do you do? You hover outside her door, meal tray in hand. "If you eat a little, you'll feel better," you call in tentatively.

"Go away! I don't want any dinner!" she yells in a muffled tone through the closed door.

That's because right now she doesn't *want* to feel better. She wants to feel what she feels, which is angry, betrayed, and sad. Until she's done feeling those feelings, she won't want anything you put on that food tray. That includes the dessert you slaved over to make her feel better.

Parents try too hard to wave the magic wand. When a child is feeling discouraged, the best thing to do is acknowledge what you see. "I can tell you're feeling really down right now. If you ever want to share with me what's going on, I'll listen. And if you're not ready, that's okay too. You need time to process whatever happened to you." Then you turn and walk away. You allow your child to seek you out when she's ready.

Now that's respectful behavior.

Every human being has bad moments, bad days, even bad months where they'll be discouraged. But don't be quick to jump to the potential label of depression.

Clinical depression is almost always accompanied by severe changes in mood, personality, behavior, dress, and grades. It's a pattern, not a one-time or two-time event. If your normally effervescent child turns quiet, isolates herself night after night in her room, doesn't pick up her friends' calls and texts, forgets to shower, doesn't seem to care about her cat anymore, and starts to slide in her grades, those are signals that she needs help. She's stopped caring about life and herself due to some hit she's experienced. That child needs professional assistance as fast as you can get her there.

> Clinical depression is almost always accompanied by severe changes in mood, personality, behavior, dress, and grades. It's a pattern, not a one-time or two-time event.

I'd always start, though, with a visit to your family physician. Because of all the hormonal changes going on in your child's growing body, your physician can run tests to see if her emotional low is a result of that. If so, it can be easily rectified. Other times that physician may refer you to a professional psychologist or psychiatrist.

A psychologist is someone like me, who can talk with your child about the issues happening in her life that are causing her to feel depressed. A psychiatrist is a medical doctor who can evaluate what types of medication could help her get back to emotional and mental wellness.

Some parents immediately rush their kid to counseling if they think the kid is discouraged. However, in most cases it's not the kid who should go, it's the parent. The parent is the one who needs the advice about how to do things differently in their responses to their child.

The majority of children who are experiencing depression tell me that their parents don't listen to them, don't understand them, and don't take them seriously. Their parents do too much for them or too little for them. Because there is no established, comfortable relationship between parent and child, the child must deal with any hardships on their own.

Many parents make appointments with counselors based on their own guilt. Typical comments I hear are:

"I had no idea he felt like this until . . . "

"I should have known."

"I wish he'd talk to me, but . . ."

"If only I hadn't gone on that business trip, he'd . . ."

But counseling isn't the cure-all parents think it is. They should have saved their time and money, because they accomplish nothing with their child. Yes, if a child is clinically depressed, she needs the help that medicine can give to get back on an even keel. But medicine alone won't fix the situation. The specific internal hurt issues need to be resolved.

Why is your child feeling discouraged? What issues is she coping with but not handling well? What is causing her so much stress that she's shutting down emotionally?

Until those issues are identified and steps are taken to learn how both parent and child can better handle them, no medicine in the world will be effective.

Eating Disorders

Anorexia nervosa, also known simply as *anorexia*, is a psychological disorder that's characterized by an obsessive desire to lose weight by refusing to eat. *Bulimia nervosa,* also known simply as *bulimia,* is a psychological disorder in which a large quantity of food is consumed in a short period, with feelings of guilt and shame following.

A person with anorexia has a distorted body image. She looks in the mirror and sees a fat person even if she's only 100 pounds. A person who has bulimia is caught in the cycle of binge eating (eating a whole pan of brownies, for instance), and then may follow it by purging (self-induced vomiting), using laxatives or diuretics, fasting, or excessively exercising in an effort to avoid gaining weight. Such behaviors take the already tumultuous teenager on a roller-coaster ride of physical and emotional ups and downs.

Though most who suffer from anorexia and bulimia are female, males are not immune. "Males account for an estimated 5 percent to 15 percent of patients with anorexia or bulimia and an estimated 35 percent of those with binge-eating disorder," says *NIH Medline Plus.* "Some boys with the disorder want to lose weight, while others want to gain weight or 'bulk up.' Boys who think they are too small are at a greater risk for using steroids or other dangerous drugs to increase muscle mass."[4]

With anorexia, your child may view a carrot, a leaf of lettuce, and an apple as a gourmet meal. She may even spread them throughout the day and count the calories religiously. When I was a dean of students at the University of Arizona, a female student brought up the subject of food in my office. She proudly showed me the food she was going to eat for that day—it was a tiny amount wrapped in aluminum foil. The "egg and ham" dish was a miniscule dollop of eggs the size of a pea and bits of ham dried to a point that I couldn't even recognize them. That young woman was carrying around her "feast" with her.

With bulimia, it's not uncommon for a 16-year-old to stop at Dunkin' Donuts after school, pull over in a parking lot, and wolf down a dozen donuts. Then she visits the john at the gas station on the way home to stick her fingers down her throat and make herself vomit so she can purge everything she ate. Over a period of time, such behavior takes its toll on her teeth, digestive system, body in general, and mind.

> **Perfectionism is the number one psychological trigger in children who develop eating disorders.**

With binge eating, a boy might find himself gaining 30 pounds and losing 40 pounds, then gaining 20 pounds. These wide swings can cause hormonal imbalances that affect him down the road.

An eating disorder doesn't have to do with eating as much as you might think. That's why urging a child to "eat more" or "just eat one instead of a whole pan" doesn't work. For such children, there is a wide gap between the ideal self (who they want to be) and the real self (who they are). That gap creates all sorts of emotional dissonance internally.

Perfectionism is the number one psychological trigger in children who develop eating disorders. Every child has a myopic view of herself as not being good enough. The behavior that results is self-defeating and self-punishing. Eating disorders are not a simple disease you can easily cure. You can't do it by yourself. If this is going on with your child, you need professional intervention.

Cutting

"I don't understand," the agonized mom said to me. "Why would he hurt himself on purpose?"

Her son was a cutter, and she'd unwittingly discovered his secret when he refused to wear anything but long sleeves on a hot summer day.

Are You a Flaw Picker? Take This Quiz.

- I can see the lint on the carpet across the room.
- I can always think of a better way for someone to do a project.
- I'm a perfectionist in my work.
- I like to do things myself, because then they'll be done right.
- I like to be in charge, calling the shots.
- I tend to see flaws in people before I identify their good points.
- I'm harder on myself than I am on other people.

If you answered yes to any of the above, you're a flaw picker. Although you're toughest on yourself, you also expect your kids to toe the line. But what do your perfectionism and critical eye say to your kids? How do those translate to them? Here's what they think:

"I'll never be good enough, perfect enough, to make my parent happy."

"Anything I do is never good enough. So why bother?"

Your critical eye produces either a rebellious child who thinks, *Well, I'll show you and give you a run for your money,* or a self-defeated, lethargic child who thinks, *I can't do anything right, so I won't do anything at all. It's easier just to let my parents call the shots.*

It's time to back off, Mr. or Ms. Flaw Picker. Even if you learned your patterns from your own parents (most flaw pickers do), it doesn't mean you have to do and say what they did to your own kids.

Now that you've identified what you're doing, it is possible to change. An old dog can learn new tricks. You just have to work a little harder to unlearn old habits.

You can do it. I believe in you.

Cutting is a self-harm disorder, in which a person deliberately cuts the surface of their body to cope with emotional pain, anger, and frustration. Those who injure themselves in such a way feel a lack of control over their life. The only way to get some of that control back is to inflict physical pain on themselves. They can control how much they cut, when they cut, how far to cut. This method of pain release can become psychologically addicting, much as an addict with drugs. Children who cut do so on their wrists, forearms, even their stomachs—places you are least likely to see.

Perfectionism is the theme that runs through the lives of cutters. As with those who have eating disorders, there is a wide gap between the ideal and the real.

Though cutting is self-destructive behavior, it's also your child's secret revenge against those who control him. If he's cutting, you must ask yourself some hard questions:

"How much control do I exert over my child's life?"

"Do I expect him to be perfect?"

"Do I allow him to make his own choices? Or do I always decide what's best for him and pursue that route?"

The candid answers to these questions are often painful to any parent. But unless you identify your own tendencies and flaws, you'll be unable to help your child. When his revenge has reached the self-destructive stage in cutting, both of you need professional help. Neither of you can tackle the behavioral change and shift in thinking that need to happen to take the path back to mental, physical, and psychological wellness.

Suicide

Suicide doesn't happen only to those down-and-outers of society who look like the type. People can appear well-adjusted on the surface, like Richard Cory in the poem by Edwin Arlington Robinson,[5] yet take their own life.

A common theme from parents is, "We never saw it coming."

When parents lose a child through suicide, there's nothing I can say to heal the unfathomable hurt and the guilt they live with. I can only say humbly, "I'm sorry. I hurt for you," and give them a hug.

The act of taking your own life is a desperate, last-option move. At times a child will leave a note, but no note could ever adequately explain to a grieving parent the complete *why* of this last act.

Losing a child in a car accident or through cancer is difficult enough. The pain is intense. But losing a child through suicide is an arrow to the heart from which parents rarely recover. That's because the action was self-directed and filled with self-hate.

If cutting is a secret revenge, then suicide is the ultimate revenge. It's anger turned inward. What is the kid saying in this final act? "I couldn't express how I felt in my life because I wasn't allowed to. I couldn't solve these problems I struggled with or take on that nemesis. No one helped me. So those issues swallowed me up, and I lost the fight. I hurt so much and feel so inadequate to deal with life that I've decided to get out. I'm done."

> **Suicide is the ultimate revenge. It's anger turned inward.**

If your child dies through a disease or accident, people rally around you and grieve with you. When your child kills himself, people don't know what to say, so they sidestep the issue. From the day of burial on, they talk with you about anything except that death. They pretend like your son didn't exist. They don't do what you really want, which is to hear a wonderful memory about a time when your child touched their heart.

Any child who chooses to end his life has gone through several psychological steps to get there. First, he's tried to gain your attention in a positive way. If that failed, he tried negative behaviors to provoke you into paying attention to him. If that failed, depending on his personality, he either withdrew from you or ramped up his efforts through unacceptable behavior. In his final stage, he's decided he simply doesn't care anymore. Ending his life is far easier than living.

If the child is gunning for revenge, he may decide not only to kill himself but to take others down with him. That's the type of behavior you see in school shootings, when a kid guns down teachers and other kids and then turns the gun on himself.

If your child is showing hints of this type of discouragement, you need to get him professional help immediately. You also need to educate him to be street-smart about the following stages, particularly as he reaches the adolescent years. Such education could both save his life and help his friends.

Stage 1: Seeking attention.

Stage 2: Developing power.

Stage 3: Seeking revenge.

Stage 4: Losing hope; deciding life isn't worth living.[6]

You, parent, are in a unique position to help your child. It starts by being aware of these stages and your child's behavior, including his need for your attention. And your kids aren't the only ones who need attention. We all need to know that somebody cares about who we are and what we do. Did you know that 70 percent of people in the workforce today don't feel like anybody cares about them at their job?[7]

That's why your relationship with your child is so important. You do care about him and what he does. But he doesn't always know it. Every day you walk a fine line between helping him find solutions to his problems and not solving the problems for him.

Your child may be grappling with difficult issues right now. The best antidote to any self issues is a good relationship with you, parent. That means you are always open to listening without reacting or judging. You allow your child to drive his own life car. You aren't the backseat driver who constantly pontificates about what he should do differently or tells her where to go. Instead, you sit in the passenger seat. You are the traveling companion who points out sights along the way, gives a few tips about what to look out for, suggests she brake every once in a while, and encourages him to stop and rest when he needs it. Above all, you are solidly entrenched in that car, along for the ride.

Peers

Family is eminently important to your child. But as he grows, peer relationships also become significant. Every child wants to belong somewhere. He needs a group to identify with. Problem is, the group he finds is filled with individuals who are all looking to belong somewhere as well. That makes the peer group a tidal wave of insecurity.

Betrayal

There's a time in every kid's life where he thinks he'll never recover. The world truly has ended. That's when his peers turn on him. Peers can be particularly vicious in the hormone-group years, when BFFs have no loyalty except to becoming top dog in the peer group. Betrayal is par for the course. Cheap shots and barbs abound. That's a given for these years.

Every child will have his moments when he is the one picked on, slammed, or talked about. The question of the day is, Will he play it cool, or will he tip his hand that he's bothered by it?

There's a direct cause-and-effect in peer groups that your child needs to know about. If he tips his hand to show his vulnerability, peers will come after him like bees toward flowers . . . only with King Kong–size stingers attached.

> If he tips his hand to show his vulnerability, peers will come after him like bees toward flowers . . . only with King Kong–size stingers attached.

80

Not Everybody Is a Victim

People today are quick to jump on the bandwagon of victimization. A kid calls another kid "ugly," and the parents of the hurting kid swoop in like avenging angels and call it bullying or abuse. Such behavior, though, is what carnal kids do. It's unkind, yes, but it's typical.

When parents are quick on the draw to accuse, they pass the victim mentality on to their kids. "Oh, you poor thing. Mommy will take care of that for you. You don't have to do a thing."

But that kind of reaction isn't helpful. The peer group will always be rough. Your kid *will* get picked on. That's because children are insecure and fight for every bit of attention they can get.

It doesn't matter whether you are a different ethnicity, you're too short, or you have a zit on your forehead that day. Kids will pick on you for any reason to make themselves feel better:

"You're ugly."
"Your breath stinks."
"You're fat."
"Nobody likes you."

These sorts of comments are flung around the typical elementary school every day. They get more vicious as kids age. Since insults are so commonplace, it would be a miracle if one, two, or more didn't land on your child sometime.

So shoot straight with your kids. Tell them that they will get picked on so it isn't a surprise. It won't feel good, but they'll be prepared for an unkind world. Role-play and help them form responses ahead of time that can nip such comments in the bud. After all, it takes two to fight or play any game. If they know in advance about the possibility, it's easier to separate what's real ("Okay, so maybe I am short") from what's a lie ("Because I'm short, I'm ugly"). That takes the sting out of a lie and makes it

81

easier for your children to solve the problem for themselves, without you getting involved.

There's another aspect to victimization too. We all want to believe our kids are perfect angels and that they'd never do anything wrong. But sometimes what's being dished out to them is a result of what they dished out to the other person first. Our nature as parents is to look the other way and minimize our child's bad points or poor behavior. However, we can't help our kids in the future if we don't come to grips with the difference between what's ideal and what's real.

Ideal is that image you have in your head of the kid you want. *Real* is the kid you have—with all her quirks and messiness. You're not perfect. Neither is she.

Ignoring realities and coddling your child won't help her, nor will it solve the situation. If anything needs to change in her behavior due to this situation, tell the truth in love, then encourage her if she chooses to pursue that change. "I know you can do that. I believe in you. And then you'll dust yourself off and move on."

You can't make the change for her. That has to be her decision.

Life will sometimes hurt, and she won't always win. But the more problems she solves for herself, the more capable and competent she'll become.

I'll be blunt. Every child is capable of working you. They know your hot buttons and when and how to push them. Some kids are controlling and bossy. Things have to go their way, with their rules. They're temperamental and terrible losers. Others shy away from any stress, making you have to step up to the plate. Both behaviors are powerful and purposeful, intended to gain the edge the child wants—controlling you. You find yourself unable to say no and step into the situation to rescue him.

It truly is hard to see that elephant sitting on the couch in your own living room. Even when you do, it's tempting to look the other way. But if you enable your child's behavior, you're not helping him.

I'm always one to err on the side of believing in your kids and supporting them. But make sure that they are driving the train, not you. Yes, being in control of the train is easier. Encouraging kids to make quality choices and then take their own steps is the road less taken. But it's the road that builds character, resolve, and good decision-making abilities.

Handling little decisions is good training for the big life decisions.

Are You an Enabler? Take This Quiz.

- People tell me I have a kind heart.
- I am easily persuaded.
- I find myself tired easily from multiple demands.
- I have a lot of compassion for others.
- I tend to believe everything people say.
- I try to make everybody happy. Then I'm happy.
- I want to please others.
- I usually do what people ask.

If any combination of these factors is true for you, you're an enabler. It's also highly likely that you're a woman, since your relational nature can easily slide this direction. You go out of your way, often at your own expense, to ease the road for your child. You do things for her that she could and should do for herself. But picking up the reins and driving her horse cart is hindering her development. It's time to stop being her ultimate fixer.

Knowing that betrayal will eventually come your child's way, teach him what should stay private. It's not a bad thing to shoot straight with him. "Would you want your best friend to know that information, if she decided someday she didn't want to be your best friend? If not, then don't tell her."

Also, do a little role playing and add a bit of four-color analysis of your own. Ask your child, "If a friend said this to you, what would you say?" Such discussions make long car rides go faster, liven up dinner conversations, and forge a tighter bond between you. So why not pose potential situations? Challenge your child's thinking. Draw solutions out of him. When you act as your child's life coach in this way, you're guiding him. You're not telling him what to do.

When kids figure out what to do on their own, without micromanaging from Mom and Dad, they solidify their own value system and develop confidence and competence.

Bullying

Bullying is rampant in today's world. Anyone who is "different" can be bullied and isolated from their peers at school or in their neighborhood. However, there's a difference between kids simply being unkind because they're kids and bullying behavior. Bullying isn't a one-time event. It's a repeated set of acts over a period of time. There is inequality on one side (five kids against one, an older child versus a younger child, a bigger child against a smaller child, boy against girl). Statistics say that children who are bullied are much more likely to attempt or commit suicide.

If Your Child Is Being Bullied

If your child is being bullied, when do you step in and help, and when do you let your child fight their own battles?

First, identify with your child's feelings and validate them. "I understand how you feel about getting teased. What happened isn't right. I'm here to help. Let's talk through a plan."

Next, develop your plan, with adult backup available. When the teasing begins again, the child says firmly to the perpetrator, "Don't do that. I don't like it."

If the teasing happens again, the child says, "I asked you not to do that. I don't like it. If it happens again, I'll get a teacher or other adult involved."

The teasing happens a third time. So the child goes directly to the adult in the room to help handle the situation.

What are those actions telling the perpetrator? That the "weaker" child is not weak at all. He's not going to put up with being picked on. He'll follow through on what he says.

However, if physical harm is a possibility, an adult must step in immediately. Children shouldn't handle the situation on their own.

In today's world, it's extremely important that kids know when to fight, when to stand up for themselves, when to back away, and when to run. It used to be that two boys could meet in the alley after school and, after throwing a few punches resulting in black eyes, solve an issue. However, in today's world of knives and guns, the stakes are much higher. It's best to err on the side of getting an adult involved faster.

> **Build up your kid's strength to resolve such situations in the future, rather than tearing down his competence and confidence.**

I'd also like to suggest that you prepare your child with pocket answers they can give to verbal bullies that will throw them off course or defuse the situation. Let's say you have a child who's 13 or 14, an early adolescent. A bully is constantly ragging on him for having pimples. What could your child say to halt the verbal attack?

"You could be right. I never thought of it that way."

"Well, I may have a face only a mother could love, but I know my mother loves me."

"If my face looks like pizza, which do you prefer—pepperoni or sausage?"

It's amazing what prepared answers can do. The bully doesn't get his desired result—fear or embarrassment—so he backs off and tries to attack someone else he thinks is weaker than him and he can dominate.

If your child has been bullied, he needs:

- Immediate comfort. There's nothing worse than being bullied and feeling alone. A hug says a volume of words.
- An advocate. That means you go to school, child in tow, and tell the principal, "I want you to listen to what happened to my son." Then you turn to your child and say, "Okay, you're on." In other words, you get the principal's attention by saying, "Hey, this is important," but then you hand the reins to your child.

  Usually that doesn't happen. The parent gets angry, stomps into the school, threatens to sue the school, and talks to everyone on the planet. Instead, make this a teachable moment for your child. Build up your kid's strength to resolve such situations in the future, rather than tearing down his competence and confidence.

- To know that life moves on. "I'd do anything to change what happened," you tell your child. "That was nasty, but things like that happen in life. I was impressed, though, with how you handled it. I love you and I'm proud of you. You're a quality kid. We're going to get through this together. I believe in you, and I know you'll power through this."

  When you say words like this, you're telling your child that he can move forward from this situation. He's not stuck. You believe in him, and you've got his back. He's going to get through this and be okay.

86

If Your Child Is the Bully

A blunt conversation is in order if your child is the bully. "Why did you choose to hurt that other boy? Is it because you don't feel good about yourself, and in order to make yourself feel better, you have to hit somebody who is weaker than you?"

Sometimes a parent has to be the hard truth teller to help their hurting child learn how to relate in healthy ways to others. Bullies have low self-esteem and are terribly insecure. Only by picking on others do they feel they can establish dominance, which ensures they keep their top dog role on the food chain.

Putting others down is an immediate high. They get social attention, even if it's at the expense of someone else. Bullies are hurting kids too. They're dumb, immature, and insecure. They, like all kids, need to learn that they aren't and don't need to be the center of the universe. Other people do count in life. Other people do have feelings. There's nothing worse than being picked on in a group and having nobody stand up for you.

> **Putting others down is an immediate high.**

If your child is a bully, you need to share your disappointment directly with them. It will sting, but it's a healing sting. No child wants their parent to be upset with them.

There must be consequences for the bullying behavior. Your child needs to go eyeball to eyeball with the other child—with both sets of parents in tow—and apologize for his behavior. Then he needs to do something for that child or her family. It could be shoveling their sidewalk for a month. Or, if the bullying went far enough, there might be a legal consequence.

Don't rescue your child from the consequences of his actions. It's far better he experience them now, as a juvenile, than exhibit the same behavior when he's 18 and considered an adult. The only way to point him in the direction of behavioral change is if he's held accountable for what he's done or said.

You can be tough. You should be tough in this situation. It's the right thing to do.

Cyber-Bullying

Cyber-bullying and online stalking are on the rise. This means no child is safe as long as they have an electronic device on hand. As long as they have an email address and a phone with which to text and access the internet, they can be a target of people who intend to harm them. That means you need to be smart to ensure your child's safety as much as possible.

Teach your child the rules of online safety and what information to give and not to give. Discuss realistically with them the responsibility of having a social media account (some children are ready; some aren't).

Also, with social media, there are very few filters. You can say anything you want about anybody with few or no repercussions. Reputations are made and killed in a keystroke. The impersonal nature of the internet makes it easy to say unkind, disgusting, filthy things about others. It has raised the boldness and brazenness of viewers and commenters to an all-time high. They are saying and doing things they'd never dare do face-to-face.

Problem is, anything stated is captured forever in some form. So teach your child to think before they post. A good rule of thumb is, "Would I want my grandma to see this?" If not, it's better not to post it at all.

Some things should never be said . . . ever.

Dating and Breakups

Your daughter is 15, and all of a sudden you hear the name "Ryan." You hear it uttered again and again, several days in a row. I've got news for you. He's the newest hottie in your daughter's heart, but she hasn't told you yet. You need good radar and listening skills to pick up on some of these things.

A few days later, she's crying inconsolably on the stairs because they dated for a couple of days and then he broke up with her.

Teenage relationships are volatile and unpredictable. They appear like lightning flashes and end the same way. Because of peer pressure and the resulting drive for status, many teens today feel like they have to be part of a couple to matter and survive in the peer group. This groupthink can be devastating to those who don't have a significant other or who are ditched by that person.

Breakups seem like the end of the world when they happen. Recently my wife and I went to one of our favorite restaurants for dinner. Sande asked our server, whom we know well, "How are things going?"

The server sighed. "Well, it's not a happy house this week. My 17-year-old son's girlfriend just dumped him, and his old used car finally died. It's a one-two punch I'm not sure we're going to recover from."

We assured her that even some great heavyweight champs have been knocked to the canvas but have gotten back on their feet and won the bout.

Your child will survive even this breakup—she simply doesn't know that yet. Allow your child to grieve the end of the relationship, but assist her in seeing her uniqueness as an individual, apart from a group.

It's easier said than done, I know. But expressing compassion and real concern and saying, "I believe in you. I know this is tough, but I'm sure you can handle it. If you need help, I'll be right here" is exactly what she needs.

What she doesn't need is, "Oh dear, how could he do that to you? Just do what I say, and everything will be okay."

With dating and breakups, you have to remember, *This is not my relationship. It's my child's relationship.* Keep the tennis ball on her side of the net. If it's her relationship, she is the one who has to be accountable and responsible for what happens to it, good or bad.

> Sharing your stories can accomplish what preaching never can.

How can you help? Provide hugs, your best listening skills, and favorite foods. Most of all, tell her stories. She may initially roll her eyes about your story of when your old BFF left you in the dust because she started dating the guy you liked. But believe me, she'll think about it when she sees that old BFF who ditched her . . . with her ex-boyfriend.

Sharing your stories can accomplish what preaching never can. Never mind their entertainment value. Laughter truly is healing medicine.

Pregnancy

Such things as pregnancy do happen. After the initial shock that you will soon be a grandmother at the tender age of 36, what's next?

It's not helpful to say things such as, "I can't believe you did this," "Why didn't you control yourself?" or, "What's the matter with you? Why didn't you use a condom?"

Condemning words will only result in a daughter who doesn't know where to go or who to turn to, or a son who blocks out any of your advice. So what do you do?

You have to have a long, hard talk with yourself first before you can help your son or daughter. You'll be asking yourself two questions, in this order:

1. What's best for this unborn child?
2. What's best for my daughter/son?

I believe the order in which you ask those questions is fundamentally important if you're going to end up doing the right thing.

The healthiest way to proceed is to get boyfriend and girlfriend in the same room with the moms and dads and have a heart-to-heart. You discuss the options. If it means putting the pros and cons on a piece of paper so everyone is clear on them, so be it.

But here's the most important point. This must be the decision of the young mom-to-be and dad-to-be. They may both be under-age, but they are the ones who created that baby. You can't be the one calling the shots. Yet that isn't usually what happens. Most of the time it's the mom-to-be who makes the decision, often with pressure from one or both of her parents.

It helps to stand back and look at the bigger picture here. I've seen how it plays out in the many families I've counseled over the years. There are generally four options, and only one of them is good.

Option 1: The young couple is forced to get married.

Option 2: The baby is aborted.

Option 3: The girl decides to keep the baby herself.

Option 4: The baby is adopted by a family who is eagerly awaiting such a gift.

Let's take a look at the options individually.

Option 1: Realistically the father of the baby often flees upon initial news of the pregnancy. If he sticks with the mother through the pregnancy, after "the big event" is over, the couple typically breaks up.

If they do go the route of getting married, they have a hard road. One or both may still be in high school. An after-school job can't pay rent, nor can a low-income job without a college diploma. Financial pressure and handling a mature relationship too early are stresses that don't make for longevity. And where will the couple live? With his parents? With her parents? Neither situation is ideal.

Can this young couple make it? Sure. But the chances are slim. What of the baby then?

Option 2: It's interesting that the United States protects the eggs of the bald eagle and spotted owl, yet we seem to have no problem aborting millions of human babies annually. I'll state my bias wholeheartedly. I believe that life starts at conception and needs to be protected.

Even if you don't believe that, take a look at all the psychological trauma that women suffer from as a result of abortions, even years later: guilt, feeling dirty, sadness, anxiety attacks, depression, grief, thoughts of suicide. The path many women face after abortion is, "Don't talk. Don't feel. Keep the secret," says author Trudy M. Johnson.[8] Thousands of women have gone through an abortion in a spur-of-the-moment decision when they hit the panic button, and they regretted it a million times. Do you really want that in the future of your daughter or your son's girlfriend?

Option 3: Some girls, especially if they're young, think of babies as dolls to play with. It's a brief journey into la-la land. But when that baby keeps her up at night, she has a difficult time finishing high school, or the baby gets ill, high school moms have few resources. Not to mention that most teenagers discover they need to have a life and want to recirculate with their friends and have fun like others their age.

She'll likely end up doing the mommy thing for a little while and then passing the baton of parenthood to . . . guess who? Her parents, who end up as parent *and* grandparent for the child. But if you're the parents, did you sign up to have a surprise baby at age 36—after you've already nearly completed rearing three others? How will you feel when your daughter gets a new boyfriend and goes off to college, and you're taking care of her 3-year-old?

Option 4: This is the clear choice from all perspectives. However, there are varying ways to do it.

Many families who choose this option—to birth the baby and grant a waiting couple the gift of a lifetime—send the pregnant teen to another state to "study," so she can have the baby there and then come home like nothing happened. It's the "secret" no one talks about.

But let me caution you. This path may sound good, because then neither set of parents nor their kids have to feel any public shame. However, this is exactly the time both families should be rallying around the young couple, supporting them.

The boy who got his girl pregnant has to stand by her. He needs to be financially involved in taking care of medical expenses. He should spend time with her and do things for her. He may be only 16 and have to juggle all these things with his sports activities, but he'll soon be a father. A dose of responsibility now will save him and you a boatload of problems later. It would also be good if he had a man-to-man talk with his parents, who can instruct him on how to prevent babies being conceived in the future.

The pregnant mom needs her family's support now more than ever, as her body changes and her emotions fluctuate. Sure, there are homes elsewhere, or a loving aunt and uncle who can help her, but no one can replace you, Mom and Dad. She needs to be in your home.

Yes, it will be uncomfortable for everyone. If she continues going to the same high school, she'll have to endure the gossip and everyone watching her belly grow. Then again, with today's social media buzz, everyone will know about her situation anyway. In years past, if you were pregnant, you wore a scarlet *P* around your neck and were kicked out of school. However, today pregnant teens are in nearly every public school system in America. In fact, special programs are designed just for them.

There are lots of wonderful organizations to assist in the adoption process. I'm very biased about one of them. It's called Kindred and is run by none other than my fourth child, Hannah Eloge, who lives in the Chicago area. She assists parents who want to adopt in making the right fit for their family. But there are literally hundreds of organizations across the country with people eager to help in a loving adoption process. Thousands upon thousands of homes and open hearts are waiting for that baby. What it takes from your end is a young couple willing to work together in being brave enough to carry that baby to full term and place him or her up for adoption, and parents willing to support that couple in their decision.

So have that conversation with both families as soon as possible. You set it up, but then agree that the parents will initially take a vow of silence. The kids should be the ones talking. Can the parents add their ideas to the conversation? Sure, but no negativity. Those teenagers need your help and your support, but it's their decision, not yours.

Why Your Kids Need *You* and No One Else Will Do

All of the issues in this chapter—Family, Self, Peers—share a common theme. Your child needs you, parent, and no one else will do.

Your relationship will change through the years as your child grows. It will particularly be stretched as your daughter or son hits the hormone-group years. Just work with the changes, keep your sense of humor, and don't give up. My books *Planet Middle School* and *Have a New Teenager by Friday* would also provide some targeted help for those years.

What will allow your kid to stay strong at his core, holding to your values, and help him overcome any hurts in his life? It's you and your support.

As a parent, you are the foundation of your child's cathedral. Upon that foundation, you are the one who places the bricks. They might be bricks of love, determination, strength, hard work, knowing right from wrong, and service to others. Your child's blueprint—her life theme—emerges along with the unique structure of her cathedral. Every child wants to count somewhere. What will her life theme be?

- "I only count when I control others and get what I want from them."
- "I only count when I please others and do what they say."
- "I only count when I serve others."
- "I only count when others serve me, when I get my own way."

If you asked your child, what would they say in response to the statement, "I only count when . . ."? Exploring the life-theme possibilities is a healthy way to look at their mind-set.

How can you best help your child with these big internal issues? You can get behind her eyes to see how she views the world—her family, herself, her peers. You can inoculate her against the issues to the best of your ability. But you can't protect her against life's hard knocks.

What matters most is that her relationship with you, her parent, stands the test of time and anything that gets slung against it. That she feels accepted and belongs in your family.

It's a funny thing. Siblings will fight like crazy, call each other names, and drive their parents up the wall enough to make them run out and buy a Kevin Leman book. But when someone from outside the family attacks one of the kids verbally, physically, or emotionally, what happens? The sibling who just called his little brother an unrecognizable name that very morning is now vigorously defending him.

Families are symbiotic. They feed off each other and support each other. They are only as strong as the weakest relationship in the family. You can't put a price tag on someone who loves you just as you are, and that's what families should be.

So give your child Vitamin E—encouragement. "You can do this and get through this."

Run together toward that fear. Don't allow it to dominate your child's life.

Be a listening post, not a flapping mouth.

And above all, focus on improving your relationship in every way possible. If your kids are safe and secure with you, they truly can overcome anything.

3

The Three Basic Fears and Their Antidotes

Understand these and you can handle any difficult situation well.

Every human being has a trio of innate fears, and those fears are interconnected. The trio is so powerful psychologically that it drives much of the way adults and children respond to life situations.

The Heavy Hitters

When you understand the three fears, as well as the antidotes you have within your power to provide, you'll be able to navigate any difficult situation with your child.

Fear #1: Rejection

Every child wants to be liked by their peers. This craving is so big that it can overpower anything else. I'm talking about a superficial

97

like that isn't in the same category as true love. I hear kids talk all the time about how many likes they have on Facebook. But those aren't grounded in anything meaningful. They're based on momentary emotion and the flick of a finger. They're tinsel-like and shallow. Emotions flare up, retreat, and blow with the wind. They make your child temporarily happy and temporarily unhappy.

> "Liking" is a temporary experience, based on who is the highest on the food chain for the day.

The same is true with liking in the peer group. "Liking" is a temporary experience, based on who is the highest on the food chain for the day. And rejection is par for the course in such an environment where every child is jockeying for position.

Yet some parents move their child out of a school because her BFF found another clique to fall into and she's unhappy. That's a classic overreaction to rejection. Just what is that action teaching their child? "When things are hard, Mom and Dad will fix it. I don't have to adjust or do anything different. My happiness is what's most important."

Those three statements have innate problems that will take your child down. First, you won't be there to fix her problems when she's 30. She's going to have to learn to deal with them herself without a hovering mama and papa.

Second, if she doesn't learn to adjust or do anything different, she'll become like a fragile porcelain jar, easily cracked. Instead, she should be like a Tupperware container—flexible enough to handle anything, even a fall to the floor.

Third, no one can always be happy. In fact, it's not good for you. As I say in my book *Have a New Kid by Friday*, "An unhappy child is a healthy child."[1]

All children are driven toward self-gratification, and parents are driven to make sure their child is always happy. Parents are even more afraid that their child will fall through the cracks and end up a social outcast. They will do almost anything to ensure that doesn't happen. When their child is rejected by anyone and the tears fall, watch what happens with most mama bears. Let's just say you don't want to run into them in the woods.

But are you always happy? Then why should your child be? Setting up a fairy-tale experience where your child is always accepted and happy actually cripples them emotionally. They can't deal with not being chosen as first violinist or first string on the team. They fall apart when their work proposal is rejected. When a dating partner rejects them, their world has effectively ended.

> **Are you always happy? Then why should your child be?**

Learning to deal with rejection is part of today's world. The sooner your child learns he'll live through it, the better.

As for you, you can't fight culture. It rules everything today. Likes on Facebook and likes in the peer group will remain huge in your adolescent's mind. Trying to say otherwise to your child is pointless right now. But you don't have to fall for the pressure of those Goliaths. Instead, you can pull a David—you can subtly beat those Goliaths with a few tricks of your own.

Fear #2: Uncertainty

We live in an uncertain world, where nearly anything can happen and frequently does. The things that keep you up at night, however, are different from the things that keep your child up. Your worries center on your job, making ends meet, and issues related to your spouse and kids. Anything that hurts those you love hurts you. You worry about your child's safety in a violent, care-only-about-yourself world.

Your child also worries. Most of his concerns, though, relate to his peer group. Even if your family isn't rolling in cash, he isn't likely thinking about what to make for the next meal or how to economize in the purchase of your refrigerator. He's wondering how to sidestep another guy who is targeting him at school for a reason he can't fathom.

If your home is tumultuous, he may have another level of concern—not only how to protect himself but also how to protect his siblings and the parent who is taking the hits.

Children are affected much more by what is directly related to them than by larger world issues. They still know what's going on elsewhere because of easy internet access, but the realities of their private existence override their wider-world concerns. All else seems free-floating unless it directly intersects with them.

Not so different from us adults, huh?

In addition, children who have faced abandonment in their early years—adopted children, kids in the system (foster care), those from divorced families or with an MIA parent, or those who have experienced the death of a parent or sibling—can feel even more that life is uncertain. After all, what they thought was initially stable (birth parents, a home life, their parents' marriage, their loved one being alive) was ripped away from them. That creates a fear that nothing is safe. At any moment, even what they have now—people and things—could be taken away.

Fear #3: Fear Itself

Every child who walks out the door and heads to their school in the morning has one fear. *I hope I'm not the one who gets picked on today—the one who gets singled out, mocked, and laughed at.*

You see, kids are so changeable that whom they target changes with the merest whiff of the wind. They can also turn vicious in an instant.

Take a flock of middle school girls, for example. Individually, they could pass as normal human beings. You might even think they look sweet and innocent. However, put them together as a group and something shocking happens. They are electrified in a gossipy, vindictive mess and become a force to be reckoned with. They instill fear into any girl who becomes their target. That's the power of the peer group.

It gets even worse because of social media that allows kids to be anonymous in their comments. Any filters of civility are often dropped because there is no consequence. You can say anything you want about anyone at any time. It's far easier to spread a rumor on the internet than it is to sit face-to-face with someone and call her a name. (However, this is changing a bit, with a few Hollywood and K-pop stars deciding to legally go after their anti-fans who take things too far.)

Because children want to be accepted as part of a group, fear rules on a daily basis. Every child—even if he is currently "popular"—is always aware that, at any minute in time, he could morph into the one with the target circle painted on his back.

If you have an only child, he may grapple with fear even more. That's because he's the only one in your family who's experiencing the hits of the peer group. He hasn't been able to watch an older sibling go through the gauntlet and survive to tell about it. Also, he feels deeply the possibility that someday he'll be alone if anything happens to you. He doesn't have siblings to count on to support him. That makes his world scary indeed.

Rejection, uncertainty, and fear itself are a part of your child's psychological makeup every day in our complicated world. He steps out your door with that trio hanging heavily on him. Much of the time these fears exist only in your child's imagination of the worst-case scenario. Other times those fears become realities. But the very fact they exist at all increases his daily stress. What can you do to ease the burden your child feels in this regard?

Three Antidotes You Have the Power to Provide

You don't always have control over what happens to your child once he's outside your nest. It's humanly impossible to be with your child 24/7, guarding him. This is even truer as he grows older and does more activities on his own, and his circle of potential contacts widens.

Still, even then, there are antidotes to the trio of fears that you can easily provide if you're aware of them.

Antidote #1: Unconditional Love and Acceptance

The antidote to rejection is unconditional love and acceptance. Your son may face some rejection in the peer group, but he can weather it all without too many dings in his spirit because he has a strong foundation of acceptance at home. He knows you love him, warts and all.

What's happening in your child's heart is far more important than what is happening in his world. In my book *The Way of the Wise*, I talk about the first six tightly packed verses of Proverbs 3. In those verses, King Solomon—the wisest person who ever lived—uses the word *heart* three times. That's how important the heart is in determining motivation and next steps. When I talk to CEOs who are working hard to realign the priorities and directions of companies, I talk about where vision comes from. They may think it comes from the head, but it actually comes from the heart.

Tough things may be going on in your child's world, but it's all meaningless if she is secure in your love and your acceptance of who she really is. She can then take rejection in stride, realizing that not everyone will like her (perhaps due to their own issues), but that doesn't change who she is at her core. She may be considered uncool for hanging out with the kid who's physically disabled or considered weird. But that's not a bad thing. It reveals her heart, which will stand the test of time in a shallow world.

A few encouraging words from you will turn that rejection on its tail and reveal it for what it is—meaningless in the long run. "I know you get picked on for being friends with Jeremy. But I think it's wonderful you see Jeremy's heart when other people only see that he's different. It shows me how genuine your heart is. Every time I see the two of you together, I smile and think, *Wow, how lucky I am to have a kid like you.*"

> A few encouraging words from you will turn that rejection on its tail and reveal it for what it is—meaningless in the long run.

Rejection won't matter as strongly if you point out that her gentle concern for others stands out from the crowd, making her unique and special. Why? Because it's diametrically opposed to what many kids do, which is think only about themselves.

Every time you say something like that to realistically encourage your child, it's like feeding pellets of love to a baby bunny. You're not only feeding her with what she needs to grow, you're also showering her with positive, healthy attention to combat the negativity of rejection.

Your words are also based on real things she does to go the extra mile for others. You're not blowing smoke by saying, "Wow, you're such a great kid." Instead, you're focusing on the acts of her thoughtful, caring nature toward others. You're not creating her self-esteem; you're subtly pointing out what she's already doing and verbally encouraging it.

With such acts your child may not get an A from her peers—at least not at this stage in her life, because they're too busy focusing on themselves—but she'll get an A in life. And that's a report card grade that will travel with her into the future and pave the path to relational success.

Antidote #2: Stability at Home

The antidote to uncertainty is stability at home. That means you believe in and stand by certain values that you've established. No matter what happens, those things won't change. When your child walks in your door, he knows what to expect. He may have had the worst day of all, but he walks into a calm environment where he can sort out his thoughts and the events that threw him a curveball. He knows you are there and you're not leaving.

> You remain the constant in your child's rapidly spinning, changing universe.

That's why, parent, no matter what is happening in your own life—work pressures, relational stresses—your child needs you to stand firmly and not blow with the wind. The feeling of instability children feel otherwise creates all kinds of emotional and physical turmoil that can last for years and impact future relationships. It's also why I tell women to never ever stay in abusive relationships. Even if you lack courage to stand up for yourself, you need to flee that environment for the sake of building a stable home for your children.

Tough things may happen in your world and in your child's world, but you're never leaving. You remain the constant in your child's rapidly spinning, changing universe. You never shift your character or your actions. You decide what basic values you will defend and not sway from, and you teach those values through both speech and role-modeling to your kids. Those things establish a rock-solid foundation that can combat any uncertainty your child faces.

Antidote #3: Realistic Encouragement and a Guarantee That Your Child Won't Be Alone

The antidote to fear is realistic encouragement and a guarantee that your child won't be alone in difficult times. "Bad things happen. I won't deny that reality. But we're all in this together, and we'll get through it. Those things I can guarantee you."

Many parents think that cushioning their children from difficult events will protect them. In fact, it accomplishes the opposite. It increases fear when those events do happen because the children have no framework for dealing with bad things.

Toni is the mom of an only child, Brandon, who became excessively clingy. The trigger was the death of a friend's parent. After experiencing bouts of this behavior, Toni realized her son didn't know how to manage his fear that something might happen to his own parents. With some tips from me, she had the following conversation with him.

"Are you afraid that something might happen to Dad or to me, since it happened to Troy's dad?"

Brandon nodded. She'd hit the nail on the head. Once the fear was out in the open, she could address it.

"What happened to Troy's dad was unexpected and really sad. Accidents sometimes happen, and people die. I know Troy loved his daddy, just like you love your daddy and me. Troy will miss him, I know. Let's think of something we can do for him when he's feeling sad."

That's the key with fears—to get them out in the open and to give them a name so you can talk about them. The bogeyman under the bed, for example, is much scarier to kids when they don't know what it is. Bringing fears out into the open is like shining a flashlight on that unnamed bogeyman. When it's identified, it's not as scary.

Note that Toni was also realistic and honest. She didn't say, "Don't worry. That will never happen to us." Then what if it did? Brandon would feel betrayed by his own mother's words.

Truth is, accidents *do* happen. They're unexpected—that's why they're called accidents. Instead of lingering on that aspect of the death, though, Toni turned the tables by suggesting they do something to help his friend. That effectively moved Brandon's focus off his own fear to a practical solution. She knew he wouldn't feel as fearful and helpless if he could actively do something to help his friend.

For older children, you can go a step further in this type of conversation. You could add, "You know, because people do die, it's so important to make the most of every day you can. Be kind to people. Tell them you love and appreciate them. Treat them well. It's also why family time is so important and special to me, and why I work hard to plan activities we can do together even when we're all busy."

Fear turned inward can be insidious. Once named, it can be put into perspective and conquered.

Now that you know the three basic fears and how you can proactively address them with your hurting child, they're not so scary after all, are they?

4

Why Grief Serves a Purpose

What your kid's behavior means and why he responds differently than you.

Anytime you experience new feelings, they can be incredibly intense. That is particularly true for children, who don't have as much experience as adults or the framework to deal with hurt and grief. Thus, the pain they feel can be even more intense and hard-hitting initially. They are also confused, since nothing like this has happened to them before. The good news is that, especially with younger children, they will often grieve for a shorter period of time.

With children, the length and depth of their grief can vary greatly, depending on their age, their personality, and the type of experience. Grief doesn't happen only when people die. It can happen as a result of any traumatic situation, including abuse, rape, a suicide attempt, bullying, and parents divorcing. It also happens when your 7-year-old is ripped away from her friends as a result of a move for your job.

With time, grief will dissipate. Life will go on. But in the midst of grief, no one wants to be told that.

Never use the expression, "You'll get over it." There is no "it"—you're talking about people and a situation. Grief is personal. You wouldn't appreciate it if someone said that to you, so why would you say that to your child? In that response, you and your child are similar. However, you can never expect a child to grieve the same way, for the same length of time, or with the same intensity you do.

With time, grief will dissipate. Life will go on. But in the midst of grief, no one wants to be told that.

Why You Grieve Differently

You and your child are two different people, at two very different stages in life. You approach life with your own unique perspectives.

Let's say Rover, the family dog, dies. He's been in your family for 12 years, and the loss hits you hard, even though you're now 34 and you knew he was near the end of his life span. You can't imagine getting another dog, because none can replace that German shepherd. He's gone through a lot of crises with you. You need time to grieve.

Your 7-year-old son, though, can't imagine life without a dog. Home isn't home without a fuzzy body to hug when he comes in the door or to follow him down the street when he plays baseball with the neighborhood boys. Your son cries when Rover doesn't come back with you from the vet's office. He has lost his best friend.

Then a day later your son shocks you by announcing at breakfast that he wants to go look for a new dog. "Can we do it today, Mom?" he asks.

You're astounded. *How can he get over his grief so fast? I thought he loved that dog.*

Some children get over their grief swiftly and move on. They have accepted the reality of what happened, within their frame of reference. Some want to talk about what happened in order to process it. They pepper you with questions and what-ifs, nearly driving you crazy. Yet others want to retreat and need time alone.

It's the same with adults, only adults hold on to grief and hurting for a lot longer. Their processing is more complicated as they deal with more angles of the experience. They think about not only how the experience affects them personally but also how it affects others.

Children tend to focus on what is currently in front of them. Usually the younger the child, the faster and easier he'll deal with hurt and grief. Younger children will get sad after the fact only if they are reminded of the hurt. Older children may still harbor the hurt deep inside, but they are less likely to talk about it.

The key is knowing your child well enough to understand what he needs for handling his grief and hurt in a healthy way that is uniquely suited to him. But in general, a child's grief is short-lived and more focused on one aspect of the event rather than the whole picture, unlike an adult.

The Purposive Nature of Grief

There's something you may not know about your hurting child. Yes, he is grieving. What happened to him wasn't nice or fair. But the corresponding follow-up behavior you're seeing—the withdrawal, the shoulder slump, the tears, the self-deprecating comments—is a *purposeful* response.

Purposive behavior, a psychological term from the Adlerian model of individual psychology, simply means that any person engages in social behavior to serve a purpose that's consistent with their self-image. That includes your child. He is exhibiting those behaviors in front of you because doing so pays off.

Seven Realities Kids Need to Face . . . for Their Own Good

- Bad things happen, even to good people.
- Life isn't always fair.
- You have to live with the hand you're dealt.
- You aren't the only person on the planet.
- Facing hardships together is better than trying to go it solo. Two are stronger than one. We can face anything together.
- B doesn't happen before A is completed. We're going to finish what we started.
- Your attitude *does* make all the difference in whether you'll win or lose in life.

The Attention Getter

Every human being's instinctive number one goal is to get attention. We all exit the womb with the intention of garnering as much attention as we can.

If you don't believe me, think about a newborn baby. What's the first thing that child does? Cry. But he's smarter than you give him credit for. Soon he figures out, *Hey, this crying thing gets those big people's attention, and I get what I want.* He's smart enough to learn to turn on the waterworks at will.

Feel a hunger pang? Cry and Mom hurries to feed you.

Diaper feels a little soggy and uncomfortable? Cry and Dad comes running to change it.

Don't like being alone in that crib and want some comfort? Cry and Mom rushes in to snuggle you against her warm, cushy body. It's far better than that cold, hard crib any day.

As your child has grown older and even smarter, he's tried out different behaviors to see what evokes the most response from you. He can now get you to fight on his behalf, spend time with him on his terms, and do something for him that he doesn't want to do. In other words, he's workin' ya, and you've fallen for it.

Because every child craves attention, he will work hard to get it. His life mantra has become "I only count when I'm noticed and the center of attention."

If he doesn't get you to focus on him and give him kudos for doing positive things—like helping the next-door granny up the stairs with her groceries—he'll try negative things. He will *make* you pay attention. He'll decide to use the power he's gained from watching your responses to work you even more.

That's when an attention-seeking child becomes a power-driven child.

The Power-Driven Child

This child's mantra becomes "I only count when others do what I say, when I control the situation."

Some of these kids are easy to identify. When life is unfair to them,

- they punch walls or people
- they have loud crying jags you can't help but notice
- they take out their frustration on their siblings
- they pass the buck of blame to others

Other kids are harder to identify but are just as powerful. For example:

- He withdraws and hides out in his room (he knows that makes you worry about his mental state).

- You tiptoe on eggshells around her because of her potential emotional explosions.
- He becomes mute, because he knows it drives you crazy not knowing what's going on in his life.
- You have to excuse her rude behavior to Grandma. "Don't mind her. She's just going through a rough time right now."

Powerful behavior can come in many forms, but it all has the same purpose—to force you to respond in such a way that you bend to your child's desires. Basically, by controlling you with their behavior, your child is saying, "Mom, Dad, I'm in charge here. I'm going to call the shots. You're going to do what I want you to do, when I want you to do it."

Where did your child learn such behavior from?

Think for a second. When someone does something nasty to you, what do you instinctively think? *Wow, that person must have had a rotten day to go after me like that. I'll give her a "Get Out of Jail Free" pass this time. It seems like she needs it.* If that's your immediate response, you're right up there with Mother Teresa and the angel Gabriel. I wish there were more people like you on the planet.

With most of us, our fight-and-nuke-'em response kicks in. We think, *Hey, you can't do this to me. I'm . . .* [your boss, your parent, the head of the PTA, or some other higher-on-the-food-chain-of-life person]. *Who are you to treat me like this?* If that's you, you're like 95 percent of humans on the planet.

Do you instantly want to put that person in her place? Bend her to your will so she'll do what you want, when you want? If so, you're a powerful person yourself. You've developed that pattern because it's worked for you in the past.

Children learn by watching their parents. What has your child learned by watching you? When power meets power, the result isn't good. As your child enters the preadolescent and adolescent years, after a few power plays fly between the two of you, one of two things eventually happens. Either there's an explosion to rival that of Mount Saint Helens, or your home resembles the feel and temperature of the Arctic tundra.

Even in times of hurt and grief, it's important to respond both realistically and positively in handling the situation up front. You be the adult. You know that your child needs attention, so supply what she needs, without her being forced to move to the next stage of misbehavior (see sidebar).

> Children learn by watching their parents. What has your child learned by watching you?

Statements like these level the playing field: "I know you're hurting. I'm sorry about what happened to you. But I've seen how well you handle life. You won't let even situations like this get you down for long. I believe in you. If there's anything I can do to help, I'm all ears. I know you're giving it your best shot. I love you."

Such wording takes only a minute, but it meets the innate need for attention and halts power plays in their tracks. Your child doesn't have to work hard to manipulate you. She already knows— you've stated outright—that you are in her court. You also are showing her respect by giving her credit to handle and resolve her own situation. And if she asks for it, you'll offer any help she wants you to give.

You've identified with her feelings but haven't rescued her or taken control of the situation. Instead, you've nudged her toward resolving the situation herself. Many times when your child is hurting, such an approach works wonders in boosting her self-worth and ability to overcome even more difficult situations in the future.

You won't always be there to solve your child's problems. The sooner she learns how to manage stressful events, the better. That means you are there to walk with her through the next steps, but you don't call the shots.

However, in situations of danger—abuse, anorexia, suicide, etc.—your parental role changes. You need to take control of the situation immediately.

Some of you may already be experiencing the next stages, when the ante is upped. If your child has been hurt long enough—for example, bullied continually at school—he may move to the revenge stage. The child who is consumed with revenge thinks, *I've been hurt by life. I only matter if I can win, dominate others, and hurt them as much as they've hurt me.* This is the stage at which a child who is abused or bullied can become an abuser or a bully himself.

But it is the fourth stage—display of inadequacy or assumed disability—that is the most dangerous for children. They are passive in life, living out the mantra "Because I'm no good and can't do anything right and nothing goes my way, I won't do anything at all."

These last two stages are when suicide attempts are possible.

In stage 3 a suicide attempt is the ultimate revenge. The child often leaves a note, explaining why he did what he did. It might be filled with self-blame and self-hate, but often it is full of blame for those who didn't understand his pain. That note is his attempt to say, "Take that. I'll get back at you if it's the last thing I do."

But when a child reaches stage 4, the suicide attempt is more likely to be well thought out and permanent. If he doesn't care about life and doesn't think he matters in the universe, what indeed is the reason for living? That person is likely to choose a suicide attempt from which there is no return. He's been so beaten up by life that he's given up.

How to Handle Grief in a Healthy Way

I'll never forget what a friend of mine did at my dad's funeral. He didn't say a word, but I knew he cared by the way he touched me and the look he gave me. It was exactly what I needed at that point in time.

A week later, that same friend called me and said, "I know this is a tough time for you, but I wanted to know if it would work to have breakfast, lunch, or dinner together this weekend. I'd love to see you."

That friend knew me well. He also knew that after the hubbub of death and the funeral details, an empty loneliness would settle in, and I'd miss my father. He wanted me to know he cared and that he was willing to accompany me on the journey.

That's how people who really know you and the cycle of grief respond. They allow you to feel the hurt, to grieve, and they don't try to explain it away or smooth it over. Then they follow up to see how you're doing. Your child craves the same response from you.

What are some healthy ways to help children process their grief?

The Four Goals of Misbehavior[1]

Stage 1: Attention. "I only count when I'm being noticed or served."

Stage 2: Power. "I only count when you do what I want or I can do what I want."

These first two levels represent 99 percent of children who are hurting.

Stage 3: Revenge. "I only count if I can hurt others as I've been hurt by life."

Stage 4: Display of inadequacy / assumed disability. "I can't do anything right, so I won't try to do anything at all. I'm no good."

Follow the child's lead.

Some children naturally want to talk about the deceased person or pet. Others don't. Some need a hug. Others don't want to be touched at the height of their grieving. Some need a quiet place to think or cry outside of others' view.

What are your child's normal patterns of behavior? Is she verbal? Does he like physical affirmation? Does she retreat to think things over? Then likely those are ways your child will also initially respond to hurt, because they can grapple with grief within their comfort zone.

If your child isn't naturally talkative, you can still support him in this trauma. But do it his way. For example, the two of you could plant Grandma's favorite flowers under your kitchen window. Even years later, you'll see them blooming, think of how much she'd enjoy them, and smile, remembering her.

Recall the heartwarming moments.

One of the most difficult things for grieving people is having someone suddenly disappear. Many times adults don't talk about the deceased person around their kid for fear that their kid will cry. But what's wrong with tears? They are cleansing and healing. So talk about the person. Share your memories of when they made you laugh and made a difference in your life.

If you avoid talking for fear it'll bring up bad feelings, you're barking up the wrong tree. You aren't helping anyone. You're avoiding the obvious—the elephant sitting on the couch in your living room. You're doing the soft-shoe dance to entertain your child so he won't feel sad.

However, by doing so you're setting up the idea that it's wrong to feel sad or bad, and that people are only important when they're alive and can contribute to you. Instead, it's good to talk about feelings and experiences you've had with those who have left this earth.

The next time your child says, "I miss Grandma," what will you say?

Try, "You know what? I miss Grandma too. When you think of her, what's the first thing you think of?"

"Her apple pie!" your child says.

"Oh my goodness, Grandma made the best apple pie. Remember when she was bringing us a warm apple pie and she dropped it in the driveway?"

You both giggle.

What are you doing? You're keeping Grandma alive in your child's memory. Someday your grown-up kid will remind you of that story. He may even roll up his sleeves and make Grandma's apple pie for his family.

Even though it's been many years since my father passed away, I still miss him at times. I can still replicate his voice and all the crazy one-liners he said. Every April 25, which was his birthday, I call my older brother and sister and talk in my dad's voice. They laugh like crazy . . . and sometimes we even cry while we remember. It's a healthy, wonderful way to celebrate my dad and keep him alive in our memories.

Be real about your own feelings.

When you're missing that mom of yours, don't sidestep your own grief for fear of upsetting your child. Instead, when your child asks, "What's wrong, Mom?" say, "I'm just missing Grandma right now."

Covering up sadness is never good long-term. Allowing the sadness to run its course is much better. Also, since grief is cyclical—especially in older kids and adults—realize that it can circle back when even small events trigger memories of the deceased person. To this day, I can't help but get teary-eyed and

The next time your child says, "I miss Grandma," what will you say?

think about my mother every time I have tomato soup. No one could make it like she did. It might have been regular Campbell's soup out of the can, but she added a pat of butter and served it to me with a mother's love. Everything tasted better because my mom made it for me.

When you lose people close to you, grief doesn't end cleanly. But the intensity of it wanes over time. That's when the feeling of being alone can creep in, if others don't share that burden with you.

Covering up sadness is never good long-term.

If you are real about your own emotions, you give your child the permission to be real as well. You build the kind of relationship in which your child can talk to you about anything. Someday your child may surprise you with how well she understands you and supports you in a time of grief.

My friend Carlee experienced such a moment recently with her 17-year-old daughter. The two have developed a close, supportive relationship over the years, likely because they've weathered fairly rough storms that have hit them together. After Carlee's father died, she went into steely overdrive, trying to catch up on numerous projects at home and work.

One day out of the blue, the grief she'd tried to keep hidden hit when she and her daughter were running a routine errand. What did that wise daughter do? She didn't say anything. She simply pulled the car over into a parking lot and held her mother as she cried.

Where had that 17-year-old learned the empathetic pattern of handling grief? From her mother. Both are strong individuals who don't let emotions fly easily. They've had to be tough due to life circumstances and being in the public eye. But both are secure enough in each other's love that they can be real about their feelings in front of each other.

Model being real. If you don't, your child can never risk being real with you.

Look at pictures.

When your child is feeling sad, suggest he take out a picture of the deceased person and talk to it.

"If he does that, he might start crying," you say.

So what? Isn't it better to cry in the safety of your home? It's far worse to let sadness fester until it becomes bitterness and then morphs to anger that flares when you least expect it.

Tears are refreshing. That's why there's a product called Liqui-Tears. When you have dry eyes, you put a few drops in and the dryness clears up. You feel much better. It's the same way psychologically in times of grief. Sometimes you need some LiquiTears to release the tension. Your kids do too.

So go ahead and cry. In fact, it's best if you do it together. Throw a hug or two in there too.

5

Getting behind Your Child's Eyes

Discover how your child views herself and how you can better connect with her.

Every single person has a way they view life. We each interpret life through our own personalities, backgrounds, and experiences. That's why three kids who grow up in the same family can respond very differently to the same event.

How you respond to your child affects their perspective when they hurt. Following are three basic types of parental responses. Which one most closely aligns to you?

Parent Response #1

Do you usually:

- try to fix things that don't go right for your child?
- do your child's homework when he has too much?

- have to tell your child more than once to do an assigned chore, like feeding the dog?
- praise your child for anything she does?

If so, you've taught your child that you'll smooth her pathway in life and rescue her no matter what happens to her. She will be ill prepared for any inevitable hardship that comes her way. When Mom and Dad aren't there to rescue her, she'll easily crumble.

This is how your child views herself:

- I guess I'm stupid because they have to tell me things twice.
- I must not be good at anything. They think I can't do anything myself.
- Do they think I'll fall for all that praise? I know I'm not the best at that.

What's wrong with praising your daughter for things she does? The problem is in what's implied: she's loved *only* if she does something, not simply because of who she is—a treasured member of your family. That tells her she is loved conditionally, based on her behavior. If she doesn't perform, you won't love her.

Ouch.

Is that really the truth? Do you love your child conditionally like that? Or do you love her because she's your child?

Conditional love means your child will never tell you honestly what's going on in her life because she fears you won't accept her if she does. Unconditional love means you accept her no matter what. That provides security in a tumultuous world.

The next time you're tempted to *praise* your child for something she does, *encourage* her instead. "I know it was hard for you to go back to school after what happened. But I'm so proud of you that you decided to buck up and go anyway. It had to feel good to hold your head high and not let those kids get the best of you."

Now that's a positive arrow that flies directly into your child's heart and lodges there.

Parent Response #2

Are you usually:

- hard on your son when he makes a mistake?
- determined to make your daughter tough so she can stand strong when she's on her own?
- pushing your child to excel so he doesn't get left behind?
- careful to control what she does and where she goes?
- sparse on praising achievements, because you don't think he needs it (and you didn't get it from your parents either)?

If so, you've taught your child that he has to be perfect to be loved and accepted. It will be hard for him to admit to you that anything bad has happened to him (whether it's his fault or not). He's afraid of disappointing you and not meeting your expectations. He longs for your praise, so he doesn't dare share with you any imperfections that might mar your view of him.

This is how your child views himself:

- If I make a mistake, I'm worthless.
- If I show weakness in any way, I better not admit to it. Being weak is bad.
- If I'm not perfect, they won't love me.
- If I tell him I went there, he'll say what happened was my fault for not obeying his rules.
- I don't dare tell them anything about this situation. I'll have to get through it myself.

Don't you want your child to push hard to succeed? Of course, that's every parent's dream. But not all children are self-motivated to the same degree. Those who are self-motivated don't need parental pressure. They're already pushing themselves enough. And being hard on kids who aren't as motivated usually backfires. They go the opposite way to spite you, and they clam up. You can't get anything out of them.

It's time to nip that perfectionistic, critical eye in the bud. It might work well for your accounting or architectural job, but it'll kill your relationship with your kids. So will trying to control their every move.

When they're hurting, they'll flee toward their bedrooms rather than admit to you that their life isn't perfect.

You can start to turn your relationship around with a few honest, vulnerable words. "In the past I've pushed you really hard. I know that. That was unkind and unfair of me. I realize now that I did it because my parents did the same thing to me. But that doesn't make what I did right. I'm sorry that I've made things hard on you. I'd like to come alongside you in this situation if you'll let me. And I'd like to ask you to forgive me for what I've done in the past. If you'll help me, I'd like to change the way I react when you tell me hard things. I promise to keep my mouth shut and listen. I'd appreciate it if you'd give me a chance. I really do love you."

It's humbling to say those kinds of things. But isn't your long-term relationship with your child worth the initial short-term embarrassment?

Parent Response #3

Do you usually:

- believe what your daughter says to be true?
- expect your child to follow through on what he says he'll do?

- treat your child as smart, competent, and able to make her own decisions?
- not think of checking up on your child, since you know he's got this?
- treat your child's opinion as valid and valuable, even if you don't agree?

If so, you and your child are standing on a firm footing of respect. If all of the above is true, there is also likely a pretty good exchange of information happening between the two of you without you pushing for it. If this is you, you've done a terrific job as a parent thus far.

This is how your child views herself:

- If I work hard, I can accomplish a lot by myself.
- It's important for me to follow through on what I say I'll do. My parents trust me.
- I'm a trustworthy person because my parents believe what I say.
- I'm smart and competent. I can figure out even difficult situations on my own. If I can't, I'm free to ask my parents.

Wow, kudos to you for building such a wonderfully strong relationship with your child. You've done a lot of things right to get to this point. You have a child who is poised to fly because she is solidly grounded in your love and as a member of your family. She isn't likely to test boundaries—doing dumb things or going to risky places—because she has a respect for your guidelines and feels safe within them.

One quick note for you: When your child is hurting, she may not be her regular competent self. Checking in with her to see how she's coping with the situation would be a good idea so that she doesn't think she has to deal with it all herself like she's used to doing with everything else. Some happenings need parental involvement, especially if your child is in any physical danger. Keep the communication channels going, though, and you both will be fine.

❦

In summary, the first two types of parental responses are unhealthy for growing your relationship with your child. Parent #1 goes out of her way to smooth her child's path in life, making her child incompetent to deal with trouble. Parent #2 won't allow his child to be anything but perfect or he'll be disappointed. His child doesn't dare share anything negative that's happening.

The third parental response is a healthy one. Parent #3 sees the child as capable of handling life on her own and trusts her to follow through on her actions, but also to know when to ask for help. When that child does ask for help, she knows she'll be believed and supported.

How to Connect More Fully with Your Child

Now that you know about *purposive behavior*—that all behavior serves a purpose—think about how your child responds when she's hurting. You can help to turn even a difficult situation around with the following steps:

1. Identify how your child usually behaves when she faces a tough time.
2. Ask yourself, "How do I usually react when my kid is hurting?"
3. When you respond in such a way, how do you think that makes your child feel?
4. How could you respond in a more helpful way the next time your child faces a traumatic situation?

5. What changes might you see in your child's ability to cope as a result of your changed actions and outlook?

We are all creatures of habit. Change is never easy, but sometimes it's necessary and exactly what the doctor ordered. The end result will be a healthier, closer relationship with your child that will last beyond this crisis.

6

What Parents Do Wrong and Right

What kind of parent are you?

What Parents Do Wrong

Naturally you want to protect your child who's hurting. But you won't help your child if you go about assisting him the wrong way. What do parents do wrong?

They react instead of responding.

Something bad happens to your child. First, you're in shock. Then your blood starts to boil. You want a piece of flesh in revenge. What flies out of your mouth?

"She did *what* to you? How dare she do that! I'm going to . . ." You form revenge tactics immediately.

Just when a child needs calm, the parent provides more drama in a visceral reaction.

There's a big difference between *reacting* and *responding*. When the doctor says, "You had a *reaction* to your medicine," that's not good. But when she says, "You're *responding* to your medicine," that is good.

Your normal reaction will usually be over-the-top. You're wounded because your child has been wounded. That's why it's important to step back mentally from the situation. Hug your hurting child, but keep your mouth shut until you have time to think.

When you react, anything goes, and you're often sorry later. When you respond, you take time to evaluate the situation and develop a realistic battle plan, and you go forward with a cool head and determination.

Remember that your child is always watching you. What you model is what he'll follow in his own life. If you're always going off half-cocked and angry when bad things happen, your child will tend to use that as his go-to strategy too.

Reacting isn't helpful in the long run. *Responding* is.

They try to fix things for the child.

It's not unusual for parents to want to eradicate the problem themselves. They want to fix things, make the situation return to normal. However, if the child is not involved some way in the solution (age-appropriately, of course, and depending on the nature of the problem), all you're teaching her is, "There, there, dear, you don't have to do anything. Mom or Dad will fix everything for you."

That might initially sound nice and kind, but it isn't good for her long-term welfare. If you fix everything for her, how can she cope without you around? Will you be around when she's in college or has her first job?

Also, fixing everything for your child tells her, "I don't think you're capable of doing anything yourself, so I'll have to do it for you." Eradicating the problem without involving your child isn't very respectful.

I saw an example of a parent trying to run interference for her child just yesterday. When I was walking into the grocery store, a kid about 5 years old was right in front of me. Frankly, he was in my way. He was dawdling unnecessarily, walking sideways, and exploring the toys in his hand. Clearly, he wasn't paying attention to anything or anyone else around him.

The mom was quick to tug at his arm and say to me, "Oh, excuse him." She shot me an apologetic smile.

Will she be doing the same thing when he's wandering around in first grade and doesn't line up with the others at recess? "Oh, excuse him—he just doesn't know how to pay attention yet." It would have been better if she directly addressed the child: "Ethan, a man behind you is also trying to walk into the store."

If she had done so, that wandering willy-nilly child would have had a wake-up call that he and his toys aren't the only things in the universe. Addressing the situation in such a way would have been age-appropriate and the right thing to do.

> **Don't be too quick to jump in and fix the situation. It's a natural instinct, but fight that urge.**

Running interference for any child so he won't realize there's a problem or pain associated with life is never a good idea. When problems and pain crop up, your child will feel isolated, thinking, *I'm the only one in the world who ever has problems.*

Down the road, who is the one who will make decisions about how to respond when bad things happen? Your child himself. So don't be too quick to jump in and fix the situation. It's a natural instinct, but fight that urge. Instead, use this situation—as much as you don't like it—to assist your child in developing good decision-making skills.

In the Westerns I used to watch as a kid, if someone was going to have a baby, one person would say to another, "You better boil some water." Then the first person would roll up his sleeves. Two minutes later, you'd hear the cry of a baby.

That's what you do sometimes as a parent. You roll up your sleeves, dig in, and help as best you can. But you have to help that baby be born, not hinder it. Trust me, you're hindering when you do everything yourself or you do too much of it. Each person has to go through a few birth pains and experience the process step-by-step.

Part of being a parent is learning that fine balance of letting go so your child can grow emotionally. It's true in this case too.

Children who are a part of the solution to a problem develop higher self-worth and the ability to work through other issues with confidence in the future. They think, *You know what? I can deal with this. It is getting better. I'll get through it.* They become inventive with solutions the next time something similar occurs. That's because their parents treat them as competent, even in this difficult situation.

They become the children who stand up to the bullies of life, who say no to group peer pressure to do drugs. They also become the adults who can take the inevitable hard hits that come, get up, dust themselves off, and go on with determination and purpose.

They deny the situation happened.

The human mind doesn't want to believe that terrible things happened. For example, what do you do when you find out Uncle Hal, who you always trusted to babysit, molested your 11-year-old daughter in your own home while you were on a business trip?

Your first response might be, "No way. That couldn't have happened. Not Uncle Hal. He's always been so loving and good to my kids."

Denying an event happened, though, is the worst thing you can do to your 11-year-old daughter. Denial won't eradicate the

132

issue. Uncle Hal needs to be dealt with to the full extent of the law, even if he is family.

But first, your daughter needs to know that you believe what she said. You're not going to merely swipe this issue out of existence like you do with unwanted dust so your upcoming guests can't see it. No, this situation calls for a full cleansing of your house.

How you respond to your daughter's words can be a turning point in your relationship. Either she will see you as her advocate and trust you both now and in the future, or, if you sugarcoat this event in any way or try to explain it away (such as, "Well, what exactly did he do? Maybe he only meant to . . ."), your daughter will never share anything beyond trivial details with you in the future. She will cut her heart off from you.

> You need to check out the details. First and foremost, you need to *believe your child* and take action.

In any situation, you need to check out the details. Children have been known to lie. But that's not likely to happen with issues that are out of their frame of reference. So, first and foremost, you need to *believe your child* and take action.

It isn't fun to deal with real problems. In fact, it's risky. Sometimes it means we have to grow up a bit ourselves. All of us are tempted to use the defense mechanism of denial at times. However, denial is much too costly when it involves your child.

Better to buck up now, accept the reality, and spend your mental and emotional energies enveloping your child in the safety and love she needs when she's hurting.

They dismiss, negate, or deny their child's feelings.

"You shouldn't feel that way."

"It's not as bad as you think."

"Now, you know that isn't true. Remember when . . . *[you cite a time when the opposite happened].*"

Those are three of the worst responses any parent can give a hurting child. By doing so, you're unintentionally digging for scraps to toss your child's way.

Let's say your adolescent stomps in the door and says, "Everybody hates me. Nobody likes me!"

> **Feelings are feelings. They aren't right or wrong.**

You reply, "Now, you know that isn't true. Just last week, that Jimmy kid called and invited you to go to a hockey game with him."

You've effectively cut off at the knees any potential communication you could have with your son. He's going to shut his mouth tighter than a clamshell, and you won't get anything out of him about why he's so upset.

Bluntly, feelings are feelings. They aren't right or wrong. Let your child feel hurt, angry, or like an outcast if that's his current situation. If he can't express those emotions in front of you, what will he do with them? Bottle them up until there's a big blowup sometime? Is that really what you want?

Many shrinks have made a living on helping people get in touch with their feelings. "If you get in touch with your feelings," they say, "you're going to be okay. You'll know the right thing to do."

Let me caution you for a minute. When your child is hurt by a life event or accused by another human being, if you as the parent get in touch with your feelings, you're going to kill the other person and go to the state penitentiary.

You can't just follow your feelings. You have to think things through first.

A lot of us aren't comfortable feeling emotion, much less talking about it. Feelings are messy. We have a hard time controlling them, so many of us keep mum. In fact, while traveling recently, I sat in a diner and watched a middle-aged couple having breakfast together. Not a word was exchanged between them for the entire meal. What a sterile, emotionally bereft relationship.

That kind of environment is one you'll create in your family if you deny, dismiss, or negate your child's feelings.

However, if we simply wait until the pressure from all our squashed-down feelings builds up so much that we explode, that's not good either.

The better way is to allow your child to express how she feels in her current situation. Her feelings are just that—her feelings. Don't take the ownership of them away from her, or she'll resent you and withdraw. Instead, accept them as her feelings and listen to her. If you do, you pave the way to also talking about solutions to her current situation . . . together.

They expect their child to respond the same way they would.

When a difficult situation happens, it's normal to expect the hurting person to respond the same way you would. But you have to understand that your child is not a clone of you, as much as you think she is. Every person responds to the same stimuli differently, due to temperament, personality, and background. When facing hurt, one child might run to a corner, cower, and whimper. Another might shout back at the offending party. Another might fight back. Yet another might give the offending party the stink eye and go about his business as if the offender doesn't exist.

Let's say you spend several years caring for your parents in your home. Your kids are very involved with their grandparents and close to them.

When Grandpa passes away, you, Mom, are understandably sad. You had a great relationship with your father, and you miss him. You find yourself frequently in tears. One of your children—the more dramatic, expressive one—responds in a similar way. You grieve together.

But your other one becomes more stoic and grown-up. She stays even-keeled, helps you more in the kitchen, offers to run errands, and spends more time with her grandmother. You worry about her because you wonder if she's processing her grief.

Actually, she is doing fine handling the grief on her own. She's the logical one who is older, has experienced more loss, and realized a long time ago that Grandpa's time on earth was short. She spent time loving him and has no regrets. She's more concerned about the grief she's seeing in you, and that you—usually the strong one in the family—are visibly hurting. Her caretaking urge toward you has kicked in. She wants to make sure you're doing all right.

You might see her as unemotional. However, she's a steady young lady who learned early on, through several traumatic experiences and a boatload of hurt, how to handle life's hard knocks. That's why she is able to sail through this death of a loved one with a broad perspective, even at the ripe ol' age of 15.

Can such a perspective truly happen? Yes. The scenario I just shared with you is a true one about a family I know. If every young person was as well-adjusted as that teenager, the world would be much better off.

Your child can get to such a place too, with some wise shepherding from you.

They play favorites.

It's a parental instinct that goes back to the beginning of time—playing favorites. Clearly, Abel was the favored son, but because of favoritism, jealousy reared its head. We all know how well that little episode turned out. Sibling rivalry and favoritism went terribly wrong and turned into murder. It caused a wide rift in humanity that still exists today.

But sibling rivalry isn't the only area where parents play favorites. It's normal to identify with the child who is the same birth order as you.

If you're a firstborn, then you identify with and tend to overprotect the firstborn child in your family. You know what it's like to be the guinea pig of the family and to have everyone overreact when something happens to you. You also know what it's like to take the brunt of your parent's critical eye if anything goes wrong. You are the one most likely to take the blame for your siblings' misbehavior.

> **It's normal to identify with the child who is the same birth order as you.**

If you're the middleborn, you identify with and tend to overprotect your middleborn child. You know what it's like to have to play mediator between your peers and siblings—you're very good at negotiating and walking that fine line keeping warring parties from killing each other. You also get tired of hearing about your older sibling's achievements and think the baby of the family gets away with everything. (You're right—he does. Take it from one who knows.) You don't want to compete with anybody. You merely want everyone to be happy, the roads of life to be smooth, and to go about your own way—one that's very different from your firstborn sibling.

If you're the baby of the family, you identify with and tend to overprotect your baby. You know what it's like to be treated as incompetent since you're the youngest. You also are masterful at manipulating your parents and siblings to do what you don't want to do. You like to be the center of attention, so you can take full advantage of a stressful situation. You can role-play your hurt quite well.

If you realize that you tend to identify with the same birth order as your child (see *The Birth Order Book* for more information), you understand why that child annoys you the most *and* pulls at your heartstrings the most. When that child hurts, you feel it more personally.

They are creatures of habit.

Scenarios tend to repeat themselves, and so do people. We are creatures of habit. If we're used to responding one way, we continue to respond that way automatically.

Here's a good example. Your child has had a very bad day at school, where a BFF betrayed her by sharing one of her deepest secrets. You can tell something's wrong by her thundercloud expression when she slams her backpack down on the kitchen floor.

You do what you usually do. You fire questions at her to get to the problem quickly so you can help her.

"What's wrong with you?"

"Why does your face look like that?"

"Can I help?"

"That's the second day you've been grumpy. What's up?"

This series of questions shuts her down. She's dealt with words being flung around all day, and she doesn't want any questions at the moment. You've only added to the drama of her day, and she wants no part of it. It's no wonder she goes to her room and shuts the door.

You've done what she expected you'd do. It's like playing a computer game that's stuck in a loop and plays the same scenario over and over. *Groundhog Day* may make for a good movie, but in real life, such a concept is bad all around.

If the way you respond doesn't work, it's time to try something else. The next time your daughter stomps in the door, think, *Hey, this situation has happened before. How do I usually deal with it?*

You recall the previous scenario. *Ah, I see. I need to do something different to shake things up.* Otherwise, you already know what the end game will be—you standing mute in the hallway in front of your daughter's closed bedroom door. You'll be no closer to finding out what happened to make her so upset.

So you try a different tactic. Instead of asking questions, you make a simple statement. "Wow, must have been rough today at school. I can tell you look upset. If and when you want to talk about it, I'll be here. I love you."

Then you turn your back and walk away. You allow her time to experience her feelings and vent them privately. You don't poke and prod at her for information. She'll come out of her den when she feels like it.

> **If the way you respond doesn't work, it's time to try something else.**

Think about it this way: if someone tries to forcibly extract information from you, do you feel like telling them anything?

Well, no. Neither does your kid.

But if someone simply goes about her business without being nosy or pushy, yet you know she's there for you when you need her, you're much more likely to loop her in when you feel like talking, right?

Case closed. Look how smart you are. You learned this important concept on the first go-round.

Now go practice it in real life. You'll be glad you did.

What Parents Do Right

A parent is much like the conductor of a psychological orchestra or band. Though all are part of your family, each individual responds uniquely and makes different "sounds" when they're hurting. Some evoke gentle sighs, like harps or violins. Some are loud and announce their intentions, like a brass section or drums. Some flutter from place to place, like flutes or piccolos.

Even in the same situation—for example, the news of cancer in your family—each individual will respond differently. That means you'll need to respond (not react!) differently to each person, based

The Enabler Parent

- overprotects the child
- speaks for the child
- reacts to emotional outbursts
- tries to "fix" things
- makes excuses for the child's behavior
- does what the child should do for themselves

The Distant Parent

- withdraws from the child
- may deny that the situation exists
- thinks the child is mature enough to handle this on their own
- pronounces what the child should do
- dismisses feelings
- lectures instead of listens
- thinks behaviors are all passing phases

The Helpful Parent

- is authentic and honest about the truth
- listens and doesn't judge
- is compassionate, affirming, and supportive
- responds instead of reacts
- stays calm
- lets reality reign instead of parental lectures

on their age and temperament. However, there are some basic things skilled parents do right.

They listen, listen, and listen again.

One of the basic core needs we have as human beings is for others to consider us important enough to listen to us. If even one other person does so, we feel relieved, happier, and more able to deal positively and proactively with any hardship.

Wise parents excel at listening to their kids. The timing isn't always convenient. In fact, it's rarely convenient. My kids tended to want my ear right as I was about to pass out from exhaustion after traveling or I was already halfway to Sleepyville. Ironically, that was when some of my most intense periods of parenting started. However, I always propped my eyelids open at "Dad, are you sleeping?" because I knew that simple question was the precursor to an important topic. I listened because I wanted my kids to feel I understood and accepted them no matter what the situation was.

> **Part of any healing process is verbalizing what has happened.**

Because I established a pattern of listening, my kids—who now range from twenties to forties—still call me when they're facing a difficult time. They know good ol' dad may not always have the answer, but I'm a great listening post for their thoughts and potential solutions.

Part of any healing process is verbalizing what has happened. A child needs to get feelings out in the open. In other words, he needs to vent.

Think of it this way. When you blow up a balloon all the way, it becomes very tight and hard. It's easy to break because it's fragile. If you let a bit of air out, the release of pressure makes a terrible noise that causes you to flinch. However, the result is that the balloon softens and becomes more pliable.

The same principle is true with your hurting kids. When you allow your child to express his thoughts and feelings, a bit of pressure releases. What he says may make you flinch and may not be easy to hear, but your child is no longer as fragile. Some of his negative emotion about the event has been released.

When you listen to your kids, you show them that they are important. They are worth your time and energy. They are your priority. You care what they think and how they feel. Listening to them shores them up so they can pluck up their courage for the next steps in this situation.

They show empathy and compassion through touch and body language.

When your child breaks down and cries, he needs an embrace, a rub on the arm, or a pat on the shoulder. It doesn't matter whether he's 4 or 14. Even if you're not a demonstrative family (you don't hug each other often or naturally), break the mold. A gentle touch can connect your hearts in a way nothing else can. It's critical to help heal the wounds of a hurting child.

> Sometimes the best you can say is nothing. Only a hug will do.

When you touch your child, you're physically saying what words can't. *I know you're hurting. I want to share your pain. I understand this is hard for you.*

In times of grief, sometimes the best you can say is nothing. Only a hug will do. Touch says, "This isn't easy, but I'm right here with you. There are no explanations for what happened to you, but I care."

Body language, too, is important. A relaxed, open stance is an invitation for a child to share with you. Crossed arms or a tense facial expression screams, "Stay away!" An attentive, I-care-about-you look is also welcoming. You might be incredibly busy, trying to meet a deadline for work. But when your child lingers outside the door of your home office, you know she has something to say. A smart parent will swivel from her desk in the den and give that child her full attention.

They use words that model understanding, belief, acceptance, and affirmation.

Smart parents say things like:

"Oh my goodness, that had to hurt. You have to feel so bad. I can see why you're crying."

"That had to be heartbreaking. I understand why you're upset."

"I bet you couldn't believe it when it happened. It would have shocked me too."

Rather than:

"I can't believe she said that to you. How could she? Well, I'd . . ."

"When your father gets home in a few minutes, he'll know exactly what to do."

"Are you sure he really did that? He's not the kind to . . ."

The first three responses come alongside the child and provide a natural connection, so the child thinks, *Wow, Mom and Dad know what I'm up against. They get it.* The second three reactions provoke fight responses, try to take over the problem, or question the child's words.

Kids aren't dumb. They know when the odds are stacked against them, and they will suddenly become mute to protect themselves. You would too if you were them.

They allow the child to come up with their own solutions (appropriate to their age and situation).

When another child says something nasty to your child at school, it's not your problem. It's your *child's* problem. You're not technically the one in the situation. Your child is. The wise parent comes to terms with this reality, as angry as she might feel about the comment. She doesn't take over and announce the solution. "Well, what we're going to do is . . ."

The wise parent says, "Wow. I see what you mean. That would upset me too. So, what are your thoughts? What would you like to say to that person who was so mean to you?"

Doing this allows the child to brainstorm his own solutions. Some might be downright crazy or inappropriate, but don't react to them. Instead, use your active listening skills to draw a plethora of options out of your child. That kid is smarter than you think.

> The wise parent keeps herself in the background and her child in the foreground of problem solving.

The wise parent keeps herself in the background and her child in the foreground of problem solving. The parent who reacts would go over to the other kid's house and raise heck by getting into an argument with the kid's parent. But does that really solve anything? It usually ups the ante further. In today's sue-happy society, you don't want to go there. Not to mention both kids have to continue to go to the same school.

The parent thinking of the long term draws out of her kid what he already knows. "This is a really uncomfortable situation. I don't like what that kid said to me. If I don't want it to happen again, I need to say to that kid, 'What you said was hurtful, and I don't like it. Please don't say it again, or I'll have to get a teacher involved.'"

Some friends of mine have an adopted child who is of a different ethnicity. When she was in a basically all-Caucasian elementary school, one fourth-grade classmate picked on her relentlessly for being different. Her mom could have swept in like God Almighty and hammered the other kid and his parents for such comments. Instead, knowing such barbs were made out of ignorance, that mom took the high road. She decided to turn this trauma into a life lesson to strengthen her daughter's character when she was faced with prejudicial statements.

She and her young daughter came up with what they called a "1, 2, 3 Plan" together. The next time that boy made fun of the girl for being different, she'd look him straight in the eyes and use #1 of the "1, 2, 3 Plan": "What you just said isn't nice, and I don't appreciate it. Please don't say it again."

If the boy made another comment, she'd look him straight in the eyes again and employ #2: "I asked you not to make comments like that. I don't appreciate them. If you say anything like that again, I'll get a teacher involved."

If the boy didn't heed that warning and made a third pass, she'd once again look him in the eyes and employ #3: "I asked you not to make comments like that. I don't appreciate them. But since you continue to do so, I will tell Mrs. Smith and get her involved." Then she'd march straight to Mrs. Smith's desk.

Note in the "1, 2, 3 Plan" that each time the little girl looked the boy straight in the eyes as she was making her statement. She didn't back down. She stood firm but then got an authority figure involved when she needed to.

The girl did have to follow through to #3 . . . one time. The shocked boy soon realized that she meant business and wasn't playing around. Mrs. Smith did get involved, and the boy's parents were informed. He had to publicly apologize to the girl and her parents.

Interestingly, after that the boy continued to get in trouble with others because of his mouthiness. However, he never again talked to that little girl with disrespect. Although he outweighed her by a good 50 pounds, his repeated ethnic jabbing at her ended because she'd stood her ground. Instead, in a twist of irony, he became that girl's advocate. When he was around on the playground, no one dared to treat her roughly or talk bad about her.

What did that girl learn because of her wise mom? That even a petite female could defeat a much larger enemy with an action plan and a determination not to back down. Those learned skills have served that now young-adult girl well all the way through high school. Though she's only a 100-pounder, she holds her own as a respected leader among her peers.

Guess where that track started? When she was in fourth grade, with that initial situation.

Now if there had been physical violence involved—shoving, pushing, guns, knives—I would have advised that mom differently. I would say, "Get the teacher and school administration involved right away. Don't return to school until action is taken."

However, in most situations, coaching a child to solve her own problems is exactly what the doctor ordered. It isn't comfortable for either parent or child, and we all tend to avoid situations that are uncomfortable. But none of us would improve in any way if we weren't nudged.

Kudos to that mom and daughter who hung in there when the going was rough. You can too.

Especially for Parents of Faith

If you're a person of faith, you understand well when I say this: Without God Almighty in your life, you will lack motivation, purpose, and meaning. You will lack hope that things can change in your situation. You will be unable to forgive yourself and others. That's because an essential piece of the puzzle of *you* is missing—the one at the center you were created to have. Without a personal relationship with God, nothing in this life makes much sense. You will feel aimless.

I know well what that aimlessness feels like. That was me, until God got ahold of me in my early twenties.

I was always up to something as a child, and church wasn't an exception. Even when I was just 3 years old, I would get away from my mother. She used to say that she could follow my path around the sanctuary as I traveled like a mole under the pews. She could tell exactly where I was by which people were looking down at the floor. To make it even more fun, frequently women would take their shoes off—I suspect because their feet hurt. Even at that young age I was enterprising enough to think, *Wouldn't it be funny if I took those black shoes in aisle 4 and swapped them with the brown shoes in aisle 3?*

At church camp, I was asked to be an usher at an evening service. So a buddy and I sneaked into the worship tent, found the worship plates, and hid them. When we were called up to serve and the pastor looked under the pulpit for those plates, they weren't there. We simply stood there, innocent as angels, waiting for those plates. Nobody ever knew at that time that it was us who took them.

In high school, I'd stay in the balcony at church with the youth group just long enough for my mother to peek up from her spot down below, make sure I was there, and smile. She had no idea what else I did during those times, and I won't tell you either.

When I was in college—the only one I could get in, by the way, due to my antics and a poor academic record in high school—chapel was required. I hated every minute of it. I had to sit in a specific chair since someone took attendance. There were 36 songs in the songbook, and a theology student would pick two songs to sing, which we all had to stand for. For amusement, some of us started a game of chance. We'd all put in 50 cents and pick a number. When number 8 was chosen, you'd hear 35 guys moaning and one guy saying, "Yes!" and pumping his fist in the air because he'd gained 18 bucks.

I was part of a group that played other tricks too. We hated the Christians who got up early on Sunday morning for church and therefore got the best food at the dining hall because they were in line before us. In those days, most students woke up to alarms through their radios. So we thought it would be funny if we turned off the electricity for one hour in the middle of the night.

One time we did just that. All the Christians slept in and were late for church. We non-churchgoers were first in the dining hall.

I had difficulty taking religion seriously, even at a religious school, because to me the concept was simply "out there" and not "in here"—in my heart. I also saw "religious" kids not holding up their end of the bargain. How could I believe that being a Christian was anything more than a label when the president of the religious council knocked up his girlfriend, for example?

> I once told my beloved wife, Sandra, "I'm so glad you didn't know me as a teenager." She shot back, "You're not the only one."

When I look back now, I realize that I wasn't ready to believe in God. Like many kids, I had to take a tumultuous, winding path to get there. I once told my beloved wife, Sandra, "I'm so glad you didn't know me as a teenager."

She shot back, "You're not the only one."

You see, parents, you can do all the "right" things—like my mother did—and still have a kid who goes down a different path. My mother was a staunch believer, and every day I'd see her on her hands and knees, praying for me. She had good reason to. I needed all the prayer I could get.

Your child may have a tough time believing in God right now. Or she may be rebelling against God and your religious "rules" with everything she has. She can't believe that any God could exist or care about her if he's making her face what's happening to her.

It won't work for you to become the hammer: "We've raised you like this—to go to church—and you're going to follow our rules." No person likes to be told what to do, and that includes your hurting kid. If she's facing a tough time right now, she doesn't need lectures. She needs you to stay by her side and ride out the storm with as much calm and patience as you can muster.

I once gave a gruff old coach, who usually had a two- to three-inch cigar in his mouth and a towel over his shoulder, a copy of a leadership book I did with Bill Pentak called *The Way of the Shepherd*. The next time that coach saw me at practice, he turned to his graduate assistant and gave him a sign to take over for a minute. He headed toward me and, in true football coach style, said, "Read your book. Liked it. Let me see if I have this straight: 'They don't care what you know until they know you care.'"

I was impressed that a tough coach who'd put many college players in the NFL could cite such an important point from that powerful little book.

"They don't care what you know until they know you care" is true for ballplayers, and it's true for your child too. Every hurting child wants to know that her parents care—about the situation and about her. She's already faced the hammer of the situation and is feeling bruised. Now she needs comfort and understanding. She needs your listening ear.

It also won't help for you to say, "God knows, honey. He knows that you're hurting." To your child, all that says is, "So God knows about this, huh? Then how come he's so mean? Did he make this happen or allow this to happen? How can he love me if he treats me like this?"

Fact is, bad things do happen to good people on this earth. It's been that way ever since Satan entered the Garden and maliciously destroyed Adam and Eve's perfect existence.

Some well-intentioned parents of faith also add, "It'll get better in time. God heals all our hurts. Someday you'll understand why this happened to you, and you'll be able to help others too."

What's your hurting child's response to this? She thinks, *Better in time? This is the end of the world. It'll never get better. So God let this happen and then wants to wave his magic wand and make it better? What is he anyway? Some sick kind of person? I'll never understand why this happened to me.*

Your child also doesn't have the capability right now to think about this situation helping others down the road. At her developmental stage, she is only thinking about herself and the pain she's in. That's only natural, especially when she's right in the middle of the situation.

So, parent of faith, play your cards wisely.

- Let her know you understand she's going through a tough time.
- Listen without preaching.
- Show your support in nonverbal ways (give a hug, make a favorite meal, provide time and space to heal).
- Don't throw out platitudes. They won't work. They'll only serve to make your child angry and to withdraw from God.
- Give your child a pass from faith-oriented activities for a while if she shows resistance. She may not feel like being a part of youth group activities.

If you are a churchgoing family, you may want to say, "I know it's rough right now, so we want to give you a bit of extra time by yourself. For the next four weeks, your sisters and I will go to church, but we're going to give you a little vacation. After that, you'll come with us again." Such a brief statement lets her know you understand her reticence to go to church and that she's struggling, but also that there is a timeline for when she'll join you in this family activity again.

My kids always knew that when they were under my roof, we Lemans went to church together. Once they were out on their own, they could decide themselves what they wanted to do.

The biggest thing you can do, after acknowledging your child's hurt and grief, is to get on your knees and pray for her. As the old saying goes, "Prayer changes things." I saw it frequently in my home as I was growing up. I recall it now when I think of the hours my mom spent on her knees on my behalf.

Prayer did indeed change things. It took some time, but eventually prayer won out. God Almighty entered my life and revolutionized it.

The same can happen for your child, whether now, in a year or two, or ten years down the road. Just wait with hope and anticipation.

7

Playing the Game of Life Smart

How to turn traumas into winning life moves.

Have you ever played the classic board game Life? Created way back in 1860 by Milton Bradley, it still exists today in multiple tweaked forms (our friends have the 1960s version). Every time you play that game, you can take a different path. Choose career, marriage, and even a kid or two—or stack your little car with lots of pink or blue pegs—as you speed along the game's twists and turns. You have to buy insurance—automobile, life, fire, and homeowners if you own a house. There are promissory notes (which mean you owe money) and stocks (which you like getting, as long as the market is good).

Once you get to the "Day of Reckoning," you have a big decision to make. It's easy if you've gathered lots of paper dollars along the way. You simply drive your car to "Millionaire Acres" and finish the game with a smile. If you don't have much money or you're broke, you can take a risk—throw the dice and try to become a "Millionaire Tycoon" in one fell swoop. Fail, and you'll be sent to the "Poor Farm."

Well, parent, you and your kids are playing the real-life version of that game right now. The expression "the game of life" is one I've used often with families over the years. And if there's one unchangeable fact about that game, it's that trouble *will come* your way. You don't have to go looking for it. So you have to learn how to play the game well and be smart about your moves.

You don't always have to react without thinking to what your child says. You can choose your response. "That's a great question. Let me think that through, and I'll get back to you." Or if your child says something outrageously off center, your blood pressure doesn't have to skyrocket. You can simply say, "Wow, I never thought of it that way" or "You could be right."

When you respond instead of react, you take control of the twists in your life journey, even if they aren't of your choosing. And with the following strategies, you can help to shape your child's attitudes so their traumas can turn into winning moves in their own game of life.

Best of all, these moves are completely within your power to provide.

Be Authentic and Vulnerable

Every computer has a history button to trace where the user has gone. Every relationship has a history button too. How your child responds to your efforts when he's hurting has everything to do with the type of relationship you have. Have you been real with your child? Have you allowed yourself to be vulnerable? Or are you trying too hard to be perfect, to fix everything for him?

Now is a good time to examine the history of your relationship with your child. If it isn't what you'd like it to be, you be the big person and take the first step in resolving the issues. "I know we've had more than our fair share of disagreements and fights. I know you're hurting now, and I want to come alongside you and help. But I feel like both of us are still angry about what happened last March. We never resolved it. I want to take the first step and say I acted like an idiot. I was out of line. I said things I never should have. I hurt you deeply. At that point I didn't clearly understand what you were up against. I'm glad I know now, and I'm so sorry I reacted the way I did. Would you forgive me?"

> **Flaunt your imperfections in front of your children.**

If you and your child have endured numerous clashes, no relationship can gel and move forward positively until that step is taken. Those issues need to be fixed first.

So be authentic and vulnerable. Flaunt your imperfections in front of your children. We all make fools of ourselves. Some of us, like me, do it on a daily basis. Your children already think you have life's answers in your back pocket because you're old and you're the all-knowing, all-seeing parent. Most of us want to stay that way in our kids' thinking to keep our parental edge for when we need to use it.

However, when your child is hurting, he needs a down-to-earth parent. No child wants to approach a know-it-all and share his pain. Neither will he approach someone who will say things like:

"I can't believe you got slugged. What did you do, anyway?"

"Where was your brain? Why would you go there? And now this happened."

"You're smarter than that. I've taught you better. Yet you allowed that to happen."

With those kinds of words, you won't even get to first base with a child who has been hurt. The kid will curl up in the corner and let life run over him before he listens to you again.

It's unnatural to flaunt your imperfections. People usually don't do that, because it's too risky. But when you are authentic and vulnerable, you become approachable and easy to talk to. It sets you and your child up as social equals. I'm not saying you have the same roles, because one of you is the parent and one is the child. However, you treat your child as worthy of respect and kindness. Flaunting your imperfections also puts you in a place where you can really help your son who is hurting. He will be much more receptive to any advice you have to offer. You will truly become a safe port in any psychological storm. He'll head swiftly for the calm waters you provide.

If you haven't had that type of relationship up to this point, it's time for a change. You be the adult. Go ahead. Take the plunge and say, "I'm so sorry for the way I've treated you in the past. I do love you. I haven't been good at showing you that. And my words haven't been kind either. Would you forgive me? Can we start fresh from here on?"

It's not too late for a fresh start, where you can approach each other with acceptance and mutual respect.

Tell Stories

If you ever want a child to learn a lesson well, tell it in the form of a story. Kids love to hear stories about your growing-up years. They want to hear them over and over. Some of the stories you tell will include bold truths about the difficulties you faced. They should include times you made good choices as a result of being hurt, and occasions you chose to act unwisely when you were upset.

Be especially honest about times you failed. Your child already sees you as invincible because you're her parent. You're older and wiser, even if your child would never admit that out loud. But you'll be unrelatable, untouchable, and unapproachable if you're too perfect. In other words, every story doesn't have to have a happy ending.

I remember well an event that occurred when I was 19. At the time I was a college baseball player getting ready for a game against Illinois Wesleyan University. We were to leave early in the morning since we had to drive from Chicago to Bloomington.

I showed up at the locker room at 8:00 a.m. and started to pack my travel bag. Just then our coach, Royner Greene, walked by my locker. A teammate was on either side of me at his locker.

Coach Greene said, "Leman, I don't think we're going to need you today." After those few words, he walked on by.

What the coach was saying was I wouldn't be traveling with the team that day. I was devastated and embarrassed. I knew the ballplayers next to me had heard what he'd said.

It wasn't until quite a few years later that I realized the guy probably didn't want to spend 10 extra bucks on the lunch smorgasbord he'd have to feed the team. He was watching his budget. Also, in those days we traveled in a 15-passenger van. If you were the sixteenth person in the pecking order, you were out of luck.

Eight Ways to Help Your Child

- Don't panic.
- Respond, don't react.
- Listen, listen, and listen again.
- Don't judge.
- Provide comfort. You are their psychological blankie.
- What you say matters. Think before you say anything.
- Stay calm.
- Communicate that you're going to get through this together.

To say the least, I didn't feel good that day. But notice that even all these years later, I still remember how to spell that coach's name. The event made a solid impact on my psyche.

What was my life lesson? Sometimes you'll be disappointed. You'll feel terribly embarrassed. But you'll live to tell about it. Someday you'll be as old as me, telling your kids and grandkids about it.

Each negative experience builds psychological muscles that will assist you in other situations. And in hindsight, it can also prompt shared laughter—the best healing drug available for any family in crisis.

Be Responsible and Smart

Being responsible and smart means you do the right thing, even when it's hard.

In most situations (abuse, rape, etc. notwithstanding), if your child has been hurt by another party, she needs to confront the person who has hurt her. That means when a cliquish group of girls has said something nasty about your daughter on Facebook, both parties need to get together, face-to-face, for a frank discussion. Your daughter has to pluck up the courage to face those girls, or she will encounter the same situation with them or another similar group. That's what psychological disclosure is all about. You're figuring out and stating why people behave the way they do. You're revealing the purposive nature of their hurtful behavior.

She needs to say to those girls point-blank, "I don't appreciate what you posted on Facebook about me. It was a very unkind act and also untrue."

Those girls need to feel the sting of their actions and the subsequent embarrassment.

But your daughter's words shouldn't end there. She needs to add, "Most of us have done unkind things in our lives. I know

people put others down when they don't feel good about themselves. Somehow putting somebody else down makes them feel
better."

It's important that your daughter be the one to say this when
the other kids are around, and that she say it nicely. She must
make it clear she knows that the other girls, who are insecure and
don't feel good about themselves, are using her as a scapegoat.
Such wording is a psychological knockout punch for these girls
in the ring.

Note again that it's *your daughter* who is
doing the talking, not you. You are there in
the room, but as a third party who is listening, not calling the directional shots.

Words are particularly effective with females, who are wordsmiths and very relational. The words your daughter chooses
to use can make a huge difference, creating
behavioral change in those who speak out
against her.

> **The words your daughter chooses to use can make a huge difference, creating behavioral change in those who speak out against her.**

However, I urge caution in confronting
males the same way. Boys by nature are much
more competitive. They tend to respond more physically and may
hit your child or pull a knife or gun on him.

Your child needs reassurance that you walk this road with him,
but he has to know that you can't do life *for* him. It's like a parent
who does his child's homework, thinking he's being helpful. Actually, he's hurting his child by doing the work for him. Sometimes
you have to support your child from the sidelines and allow him
to make the tough decisions. This is especially important as your
child gets older, when the stakes are higher.

Sometimes your child's actions need to change in order for
the outcome to change. That drama queen of yours must learn

to tone down her behavior. Your quick-to-use-his-fists son must find other ways to defuse.

Part of learning responsibility is choosing to respond rather than do what comes naturally—react. If you yourself aren't responsible with your life, how can your child learn to be that way? Sometimes you have to step up to the plate and be the adult.

Be Attentive

If you want your child to know you care, give him your undivided attention. Make contact. Put away that cell phone. Nothing is as important as this moment, when your child wants to communicate with you face-to-face.

The words you choose to use with your children make a big difference.

"I care what you think."

"Your feelings are important to me."

"I know it's really tough right now. I'll always listen."

"I can tell you're thinking things through and putting a lot of time and effort into that."

Those sorts of comments send a message to your child that he is your top priority. Work isn't as important. Your social life isn't as important. Family comes first. When your kid is hurting, you're there. It doesn't matter if the situation is messy emotionally or tough to deal with. Your support is unconditional.

Being attentive doesn't mean piling on questions. Questions won't make your child talk. In fact, they'll either shut him up or drive the quality of any conversation down.

Instead, it's important to actively listen. What do I mean by that? Listening shouldn't be a passive activity. It isn't simply sitting back, nodding your head, and saying, "Uh-huh" as the other person talks, and in the meanwhile you're formulating what you should say next. Active listening is paying intense attention—through eye contact, physical touch—and responding in some tangible way to the new information your son or daughter gives you.

If you listen like that, your child still may not be ready to talk further. But she can't help thinking, *He really cares. He understands what I'm up against.*

Active listening shows empathy and compassion and makes connections. If you want to make a difference in your kid's life, you have to be a good listener. Fortune 500 companies are built on that style of communication. Walk into any company headquarters and you won't have to look far before you see the word *communication* on a hall plaque somewhere. Successful people know how to communicate, and that includes you, parent.

> **Questions won't make your child talk. In fact, they'll either shut him up or drive the quality of any conversation down.**

When you are attentive—listening carefully, being open to your child's response but not demanding it—you are showing ultimate respect for your child as a person.

Be Positive

Life is full of lemons. You can choose whether to simply put up with their sour flavor or to add a dash of sugar and churn a delicious lemonade out of them.

However, be careful not to drown your kids in the lemonade you dish out. Don't be the overly optimistic Pollyanna who offers something sticky-sweet and unpalatable. Your kids aren't going to fall for it.

Be Comfortable

My wife rolls her eyes frequently when she sees me watching an episode of an old Western I grew up watching, such as *The Lone Ranger*. She can't understand why I'd want to watch that stupid old TV program again.

But I know why. When I'm tired, when I've been interacting with people all day long, sometimes I want to veg. Watching such a program reminds me of simpler times. When I was a kid, I'd sit in front of my 17-inch black-and-white TV and watch my hero cure the ills of the Wild West. It was a pure and simple pleasure. Rewatching *The Lone Ranger* rekindles my feelings of home, warmth, family, and security. It's a comfortable place to be.

> Are you the comfortable chair your child needs?

It's the same way I feel about my favorite chair. When I want to relax, it has to be in that chair. It has exactly the right support and has substance, depth, and warmth.

We humans don't gravitate toward things—or people—that make us uncomfortable. Are you the comfortable chair your child needs? Are you supportive yet not stiff? Do you have substance, depth, and warmth? If so, your child will naturally gravitate toward you and want to settle in.

If you focus on improving your relationship and keeping it strong, your child will find their comfort zone in family, and they won't be as pressured by peers or as thrown by bad things that happen.

Playing the Game of Life Smart

When your child has been thrown curveballs, you've got everything you need to be smart about your next move:

1. Expect tough times to come, because they will.

2. Keep calm and evaluate your situation. If you look at problems simply and don't make them more complicated than they are, you'll get your answer.

3. Remember, the choice is yours. You are in charge of your feelings and actions.

4. Use common sense to responsibly strategize your next moves.

5. Realize you'll have twists and turns where you can't see around the corner, but you'll eventually make it to the end in one piece.

If you follow those simple strategies and reminders, you can turn even the unlucky draws in life into winners. That's because you're always holding the ace of all aces that trumps anything else.

What is that ace? Simply stated, it's your relationship with your child.

If your child knows she belongs to you and that you're committed to playing the game of life together, she'll have lasting self-worth. She'll know she's valued just as she is, no matter what's currently happening in her life.

I guarantee it.

ASK DR. LEMAN

Q&A

Straightforward answers to key questions parents ask about dealing with difficult, real-life issues and their hurting kids.

Doesn't Fit In

Q: My almost-13-year-old daughter has been really down for the past couple of weeks. I think it's because the girls who used to hang out with her aren't anymore. Worse, some of them make nasty comments. How can I help Emma at such a low point, where she feels like she doesn't fit in, no one likes her, and she's losing friends?

A: Memo to Mom: Almost-13-year-olds can go for long periods of time feeling like they don't fit in. BFFs change with the direction of the wind. But I can guarantee that those friends who are no longer acting like BFFs feel the same way your daughter does right now—lonely and searching for somewhere to belong.

Not fitting in, switching friend groups, being mercurial—all these are common behaviors for girls that age. One of your key jobs is to take the ups and downs of that roller-coaster adolescent ride in stride, rather than charging in like an overprotective mama bear to protect your cub. (You certainly don't want to tango with any of the other protective mama bears protecting their cubs, so let the anger and defensiveness go.)

How can you help your hurting daughter? Tell her some stories about low moments you had with friends during those adolescent years (and I know you've had some—we all have—so just fess up). "Did I ever tell you about the time I was in seventh grade . . ."

Talk about times you didn't fit in, like when it first hit you that most of your friends were athletic and you couldn't tie your shoelaces without falling over. It came to a head one day when you slid into the place you usually sat at the lunch table with your girlfriends and one of them remarked in a snotty tone, "Well, if it isn't Ms. Clumsy herself joining us for lunch."

"I wanted to cry," you tell your daughter. "But instead, I said, 'Yeah, that's me. You got it right. Some people put their shoes on the wrong feet. My feet are just on the wrong legs.'"

You explain how you were fast enough to cover your hurt with humor for the moment, but later you cried at home in your bedroom. "Stuff like that really hurts," you share with her. "I mean, I still remember it now, and I'm kinda old. But you know what? That's also a time when I started to search for other friends who had interests more similar to mine. Kids who were interested in art, for example. You'll do that too."

Revealing some of your own stories tells your daughter, "Hey, I've been there. It hurts and it isn't fun, but you'll get through this."

Here's the second way you can help. Ask yourself these critical questions: "Does my daughter fit in at home? Does she know she belongs there?"

If I asked your daughter those questions, would she tell me honestly that she feels valued and loved at home? That you see her as a strong person who goes after what she wants with determination? That you believe in her?

If your daughter truly belongs in your home, and you see her in those ways, rest assured she will be okay. She'll need some hugs, some encouragement, and from time to time even a little coaching. Keep listening well, and you'll keep the conversation flowing. If you do so, you'll have the opportunity for teachable moments even in the midst of this hurt.

So first, you identify with your daughter's hurt—her feeling left out and upset that one of her girlfriends said something unkind. "Wow, no wonder you were crying," you say. "I'd cry too. I'm so sorry that happened to you. Middle school girls can be really mean sometimes, even if they are supposed to be your friends."

Then you rub her arm or give her a hug and say, "Seems like you've got a couple of choices right now, huh? You can take what she said to heart and curl up and hide out in your bedroom. Or you can gather that strength from within that I know you have . . . and keep moving forward with a smile."

Let me tell you, middle school girls can spot any hint of weakness a mile away, and they'll pounce on it. But they don't know what to do with someone who takes negative comments with a lighthearted air, replies, "Yeah, I guess you're right," and then moves on from there.

Think of it this way. Everything in life is generated from the attitudes of the heart. And those attitudes begin in the home. Is your home the centerpiece of your daughter's heart? Is she comfortable there and able to retreat for short periods during the storms of life, only to reemerge stronger?

Strength comes from within and starts with the home environment. If your daughter is solidly entrenched in the safety of your home and in your relationship, she can weather anything . . . even middle school girls. I know it, because my wife, Sande, and I have helped shepherd four daughters through that time period and lived to tell about it.

Warring Siblings

Q: My 7-year-old son is being tormented by his older sister, who's 10, and frequently runs to me, crying for help. She says he's always crying and then tries to get her in trouble, which is often the result. My husband gets upset about the two kids always fussing with each other, yells at Maggie to stop picking on her brother, and sends her to her room. Davey's often in tears in his daddy's lap. Maggie gets angry and ends up trashing her room. Every night it's the same replay, and I'm sick of it—sick of seeing the kids hurt each other, sick of hearing my husband yell. Help!

A: Those two kids have taken over your family with their dog and pony show. That "innocent" 7-year-old knows exactly what he's doing—he's playing both you and your husband.

Babies of the family can be manipulative and good at setting people up, especially their siblings. All they have to do is breathe the words "My sister is picking on me" when they run to Dad or Mom, and you'll adopt full battle gear to protect them. So you go in without knowing the full story and give Maggie a piece of your mind (or your husband does).

Did either of you ever ask, "What led Maggie to pick on you, Davey?" Chances are, he did something to annoy her and encourage that tormenting behavior.

But what do most parents say, even if the baby of the family is annoying? "I don't care what he did. You're the oldest. You ought to know better. I expect more out of you." So the older child gets put down, no matter what happened.

As soon as you make yourself judge and jury over warring siblings, you've lost in sibling rivalry. They'll just amp up the fight because they've got an audience.

Fighting is, at its core, an act of cooperation. Your kids are cooperating with each other to pick the fight and continue it. If you weren't in the room, most fights wouldn't continue because there's no fun in it without manipulating Mom or Dad.

Here's an easy way to separate the wheat from the chaff and bring civility back to your jungle-like current atmosphere. When Davey runs to you and says, "Maggie's picking on me," take a step back from the little tattletale. Raise an eyebrow and say, "Really? Well, I'm sure the two of you can work it out between you." Then walk away into another room.

Because his tactics have worked before, Davey will run after you. His pleas will get louder. You simply state, "I'm sure the two of you can work it out." Then you disappear into another room where he can't follow and shut the door.

Shocked silence will result. Those few words will take the wind right out of his sails. It'll stop the fight even before it starts.

You can also stash the two warring siblings in the same room. "You two have something to work out," you tell them. "I don't want you to leave this room until you come up with a solution to the problem together." Then you close the door and walk away.

Of course, if your kids have a tendency toward physical violence, or if one is a lot larger than the other, keep a close eye and ear on the room without them realizing it, to make sure they're both safe.

Most of the time deafening silence reigns, and both kids are sheepish and embarrassed. You might even hear a couple muffled echoes of "Sorry."

But—and here's the big one, parent—just because they ended this one sibling battle without engaging in war doesn't mean that life returns to normal. If you adopt that plan, the skirmishes will continue.

That night you say, "I'm glad the two of you were able to work that out. But I have to tell you, I'm so disappointed in you and your behavior. We'd planned to go to the water park tomorrow, but we're canceling that outing. Until the two of you learn to get along and show your father and me that you can do so, we won't do fun things like the water park."

Right now it may seem like your son is the one hurting because he's getting picked on. But don't be fooled. It's very likely your cherub got what he deserved from his sister. Yet he's counting on the fact that you'll protect and back him no matter what, so he gets away with everything. Allowing him to continue to manipulate won't help him with any relationship in the long term. Someone—you or your husband—needs to be a truth teller. "You're saying your sister picks on you a lot. What exactly are you doing that makes her want to act that way?"

Your daughter is hurting because she's always the one who gets in trouble no matter who starts the fight, because she's older. Life seems very unfair, and it is. Since she has her own part in the fight—picking on her younger brother—you need to even the playing field. Have a little conversation. "Sometimes your little brother seems over-the-top, doesn't he? He gets away with a lot, and that's not fair."

Maggie is nodding. *Hey*, she thinks, *finally someone understands me.*

Then you deliver the teachable moment. "You two get into each other's faces a lot these days. Yes, he can be a pain in the keister sometimes. But I think I know what may be going on. I could be wrong, but I'm wondering . . . do you feel bad about yourself for some reason? Is that why you have to pick on your brother—to make yourself feel better? Does picking on him and putting him down make you feel better? If so, that's not a good way to live, because putting others down won't make you feel better in the long run."

Power struggles between siblings can lead to a lot of hurt in the family unless the ball is served into the right court. If physical danger is involved, you should step in immediately. Otherwise, don't get in the middle. Let the kids solve their own problems, and those issues can disappear like wisps in the wind without you as an audience.

Don't allow yourself to be manipulated . . . especially by that charming baby in your family.

Gossip or Bullying?

Q: My 15-year-old came home from school yesterday crushed and crying. She'd seen a group chat about her:

"She's not even that pretty."

"Or that smart either."

"Guess she's got something going for her."

"Oh yeah? Like what?"

"She's only an A-cup."

"I barely even know these girls," Annalisa told me. "Why are they picking on me?"

I feel so bad for her. I didn't learn until later last night—from another mom—that the comments got much worse than that. I don't know if my daughter knows yet how bad they got. I'm burning inside, wanting to defend her. When should I step in, and when should I butt out and let her handle things?

A: There's a simple answer to the question "Why are they picking on me?" Here it is: "Because they can."

Even a step into high school makes you like a duck in the sky in hunting season. You can be completely innocent and still get targeted.

However, not every duck is completely innocent. Your daughter might be a target for a reason. Even if she doesn't know the other girls well, she might unwittingly have done something to incur the wrath of the Alpha Girl who started the chat. By that, I mean she might have looked the wrong way at the other girl's boyfriend. She might have had the audacity to say hello to him in history class, and that's what kicked off the jealousy.

Kids are stupid and jealous. Combined with teenage hormones, that can be a deadly combination in the peer group. Adolescents react at a visceral level. They'll say and do anything. The concept of "responding"—taking in information and evaluating it before acting—isn't even in their vocabulary.

But let me make something very clear. Saying your daughter isn't pretty is one thing, and it's common when every girl is competing to be that Alpha Girl. It's hurtful, yes, but it'll blow over. Those girls will find somebody else to pick on tomorrow. (Every high schooler begins her day with one prayer: "God, please let them find somebody else to pick on today.")

It's another thing to talk about bra size. That's unacceptable. But today's adolescents have never developed their filters on anything, including sexual references. I'm not surprised the group chat degraded further. I know a girl who was called a slut simply because she smiled at the most popular boy in high school. A girl who liked him started a rumor about her sleeping around with five boys on the football team.

If the conversation descends to that kind of level, it's time to rally the forces. By that, I mean you contact the school principal, explain the situation and who's involved, and calmly state and show the evidence so that the parties (kids and parents alike) can gather on neutral ground to discuss exactly what has happened and decide appropriate next steps.

In situations like this, most parents are quick to jump to the bullying bandwagon. However, for the term *bullying* to truly apply, not only does the action have to be repeated, but an inequality has to be present (for example, a much larger kid on one side, or a group against a single child). In this case, it's a group against a single child, but there's no repeated pattern between your daughter and the girl group—at least that you know of.

Here's what I'd do for now. Say gently to her, "I see how upset you are. I'd love to be able to help. But I don't have a clue how to do that until I know exactly what happened. Any background info you can give me would help. If you don't want to talk, that's okay too. I understand. But when you're ready to talk, I'm here. Come find me and I'll be all ears."

Never badger a kid to talk. Sometimes kids are reluctant to narc on each other, even if they are hurting. If your daughter doesn't want to talk, respect that wish. But be alert and ready for an opening where you can try again.

If and when your daughter decides to talk, shut your mouth and listen. You may be shocked about the details of what you hear. Kids are kids, and they'll say mean things without thinking of any consequences to themselves or others. But you don't want to be the parent in a parent/child/principal meeting who hears for the first time what *your* child did—even if minimally—to provoke Alpha Girl's wrath. If the situation escalates, you want to have all the information in your back pocket before the forces gather.

However, for now, what your daughter needs most is some TLC and a listening ear from the home front.

Retreating and Cranky

Q: I'm concerned about my 11-year-old. He's a sweet boy and very interactive. But ever since he entered middle school, he's retreated from us and become cranky. When I ask him about his day, he fires back, "Okay," then heads to his room and shuts the door. Once or twice he's smacked the wall in the hall on the way. He doesn't come out until he smells dinner.

What happened to the happy kid who always wanted hugs and used to talk nonstop after school? It's like he's completely morphed personalities. Worse, somebody else had to tell me he didn't make the football team. What's going on? Am I losing my son?

A: From your concerns and questions, I assume this is your first time around the track with an adolescent. No, you're not losing your son. This is normal behavior for an 11-year-old boy. All boys that age are working hard to figure out exactly who they are, apart from being a chick in your nest.

Boys especially face a tough, competitive world, and your son has come face-to-face with that reality. He needs a good dose of Vitamin E—encouragement—from you, especially since he's been rejected. Worse, it's a public rejection. His peers know he tried out for the football team but didn't make it. That paints a big *L* for *loser* on his forehead . . . all at a time when he's learning how to swim amid a bunch of sharks who feast on the weakest shark.

Part of becoming a young man is gaining a man's competitive edge, and your son has had the rug pulled out from under him at a critical time. Every time he sees that football team practice, his inadequacy is emblazoned right in front of him.

What can you do? Gently encourage other talents and interests that he has, such as gaming, bowling, or fixing up an old car. Spending a little money on projects like those will be way better than repairing drywall in the house after he punches holes in the hallways. Having a positive activity to focus on will help redirect his anger and discouragement. So get creative. Think about what your son enjoys.

As far as isolating himself and not wanting to talk to his parental units, welcome to the world of adolescence. Get used to it. Just be glad for the times he does want to talk, and listen up. But it doesn't mean you take guff from him either.

At this low point in his life, your son doesn't need a fake rah-rah cheerleader with pom-poms, nor does he need a hovercraft. Do yourself and him a favor. Don't ask him questions. Those only manage to shut him off.

Don't play the "fix him" game either. Most parents' knee-jerk reaction to a child getting hurt is trying to come up with a panacea, such as, "So you got cut from the football team. Maybe you could go out for bowling." There is no panacea for your son's hurt. He has to work through it himself.

Give him the time to feel the blow and lick his wounds. Acknowledge the hurt. "I can tell you're really hurt right now. If you're not ready to talk about it, that's okay. Just know I'm here if you need a listening ear." He needs your support and understanding, and to know you're in his court but not crowding him.

Sexually Active?

Q: I overheard my 14-year-old daughter talking with her friends about how to know if you're pregnant and how to get birth control pills. I admit I'm worried, especially since I married at 17 because I was pregnant with her, and my marriage didn't work out.

Melanie seems less talkative and more distracted lately too—much different than her usual bubbly self. When I try to ask her if she's upset about something, she only says, "I'm okay, Mom, don't worry." Saying "don't worry" instead of telling me what's bothering her actually worries me more, since we used to talk all the time about everything.

Any tips? I don't want her to go down the same road I did.

A: You have valid concerns. Today's teens are becoming sexually active at an early age (middle school being a prime target for sexual exploration), but most girls really don't want to get pregnant.

I say *most* girls because some who have an intense craving for love and acceptance believe that a child—someone always by their side who belongs solely to them—will provide a connection that is otherwise lacking in their lives. But such a fairy tale usually comes with the dream of a knight in shining armor also by their side.

Other girls have an intense craving for a guy's attention because they didn't have their daddy's love growing up. I call it "daddy deficit disorder"—a desire for male warmth, connection, and protection. It can be so strong that it overrides common sense.

Panicking or jumping to conclusions may be very tempting right now, but that's not the answer. Getting on your soapbox about what it's like to be a pregnant, unwed teen won't do your daughter any good, even if you were one. To truly understand a situation, you have to step directly into another person's shoes, and you don't want your daughter to be in your old shoes.

It's likely that Melanie, at age 14, has probably already had a sex ed class. That covered the basics, but middle school girls are filled with curiosity and questions. Their bodies are changing, and they're noticing the physical development of older boys. Your daughter has also been bombarded with sex ed "facts"—most of which aren't true—from her peers and the internet. Her questions might be a part of her natural research.

But there's also a possibility that your cute daughter caught the eye of a 16-year-old boy, and she might be infatuated with his attention. Put together a 14-year-old hormonal girl who is lacking a daddy's affection and a 16-year-old testosterone-laden male, and some things will happen. None of them are very good. Your daughter doesn't have enough life experience to know that yet, so you need a way of approaching her no-fly zone with appropriate conversation.

At this point if your daughter isn't asking you directly, she probably isn't open to your direct opinion or input. After all, no adolescent is interested in having knowledge of their parents' sex life. I still remember realizing, "Ew, you mean my parents really did *that* to have me?"

Of course, there are plenty of internet and magazine articles available about contraception, not to mention all the gossip she hears from her girlfriends. Giving her a lecture about being careful not to get pregnant won't do anything . . . except ruin the potential for a good discussion once she's open to talking. But you can still provide realistic, quality information to combat the myths. A well-placed magazine article or two in your reading stash in the family room isn't a bad idea. Kids are naturally voyeuristic.

Or you might casually say over hot chocolate, "Hey, it's been a long time since I was 14. But today I saw an article that made me wonder if it was true. It said 4 out of 10 eighth-grade girls have had some kind of sexual experience. Do you think that's true or not?" It's a way to open the discussion if she wants to get some input from you but doesn't know how to frame her questions.

Or you can adopt the straightforward method. "I've got to be honest with you. Last time we talked, you said, 'Don't worry about me. I'm fine.' Well, I am worried. I overheard you talking with your girlfriends about birth control pills. Since you're asking them, I think it would be wise for you and I to have a frank discussion about birth control pills. I know this isn't an easy topic to talk about for you—or for me. But you're mature enough now to have this conversation."

If she interrupts or says she has to go somewhere, you have to be firm. "Before you or I go anywhere else, we need to have this conversation. It's too important not to."

This is the principle I call "B doesn't happen until A is completed." What's more important should never get ousted by a lesser event, including shopping with a girlfriend.

So you continue. "I'm sure you've heard a lot of information about pregnancy and birth control pills. Some of it is true. Some of it is false. You deserve the best out of life, and that includes knowing the facts about birth control. I've been on it at times in my life, and I know what it's like. There are lots of forms of contraception. . . ." And you proceed to describe the different types.

You end with, "I don't know everything about this subject. If you know other things we haven't discussed, I'd love it if you'd share those facts with me. What I do know is that I love you. I want to answer questions you might have about these topics. If you choose to share those with me, I promise not to freak out or jump to any conclusions.

"This is a very critical subject for me, because you matter deeply to me. It's easy to fall for the feel-good emotions when a boy likes you. But if we all went through life just following our feelings, we'd be in trouble.

"Pregnancy is life changing. I know, because I got pregnant at 17, and the result was you. I wouldn't ever change that you are on this planet or that you're my child. But you know it hasn't been easy for either of us without a daddy. Your daddy was 17 too, and he wasn't ready to be a father.

"Nobody loves you more than me. And I want you to someday have a wonderful, loving relationship with a guy who will protect you and stay with you. You deserve that. That means you don't have to give away anything—like your virginity or even a kiss—to get love."

Your daughter may fidget in embarrassment or pretend like she didn't hear you and flee the scene as soon as she can. But trust me, she heard you. She'll be processing everything that you, the most important person to her, said . . . behind the closed doors of her bedroom.

I would also make sure to thank her for listening to you and make an admiring comment about her maturity in doing so. Because you were honest, confirmed your love for her, and didn't preach, you've kept the communication doors open. When she's ready to talk, she'll be much more likely to converse with you to get the straight scoop. And if there is an older boy with his eye on her, she's got some additional ammunition for saying no to anything other than his verbal flattery.

In today's world, a lot of kids do have a sexual experience at an early age. But just because it happens often doesn't mean it's good physically or psychologically for the parties involved. Those who say otherwise have never experienced the agonizing betrayal of a breakup or the pain and fear of an STD.

On this subject, stand firm, Mom. There's too much at stake to do otherwise.

Angry Loner

Q: My son had a good group of friends for elementary and middle school. They went to different high schools but still hung out a lot together on the weekends their freshman year, mainly creating new songs for the band that practiced—loudly!—in our garage.

That summer Ryan, Andrew's longtime best friend, committed suicide. Nobody saw it coming, and everybody was devastated. The friend group drifted apart. Andrew got mad on the first day of school and smashed the guitar he used to play.

Since then he's become a loner. It's now several months into his sophomore year, and he hasn't made new friends. He's become secretive and closemouthed. He often sits in the dark in his room.

Is this his way to work through his friend's death—or something else? How can I know? How can I help? When should I step in, and when should I allow things to run their course, to let him work out his feelings on his own?

A: Your son's had a big hit at a volatile time, so no wonder he's reeling. Losing a best friend is rough for any adolescent. He's had the same group of friends for most of his life, and then they all go different ways. Though that's a natural progression, especially between middle school and high school, parting from friends and having to make new ones isn't easy.

But the reason for the loss and Ryan's type of death make the loss even more difficult to deal with. Andrew is going through the stages of grief.

Stage 1 is disbelief: *How could this happen to me, to my friend? Why would he do something like that?* It is difficult for those who have not entertained suicidal thoughts themselves to understand how someone would be so discouraged and at the end of their rope that they no longer want to live.

Stage 2 is guilt: *How come I didn't see it coming, when he was my best friend? Could I have done anything to stop it?*

Stage 3 is anger and revenge: *How could my friend do this to me? I hate him. Life isn't fair!* That's when Andrew smashed his guitar. It was likely the link that reminded him most of his buddy and also the band and the fun times they'd had together.

Stage 4 is withdrawal: *Why try? Nothing turns out the way I want it to anyway. Everybody I love will leave me anyway. I give up.* Andrew sitting in the dark and becoming secretive and quiet are evidences of this stage. But let me note here that *all* adolescents have their times of keeping secrets from their parents and withdrawing when they feel overwhelmed. They'll also flare up if you enter their space without invitation. All that is normal hormonal teenage behavior. But if you see a continued disinterest in life, food, friends, and grades (all signs of psychological struggle), it's time to take action.

Think about how difficult it is for us as adults to grasp the devastation of a suicide of someone close to us. Now think back to when you were a teenager—that tumultuous time of hormone changes, school upheavals, friend betrayals, self-esteem hits, etc. See why it's even harder for a teenager to grapple with the suicide of a friend?

So what should you do with Andrew? It's time to sensitively step in since your son clearly shows signs of stages 3 and 4 of grief. It's one thing to be angry. It's another thing to strike out and destroy property, even if it's his own. That's way out of bounds for what's appropriate in responding to a life crisis. But you don't start by harping on him about destroying his guitar. He's probably already thought that through himself at least a time or two: *Wow, that was stupid. And I really liked playing the guitar.* Instead you start by saying, "You know, Andrew, I've been brooding about something for a while and need to talk to somebody about it. I wonder if you'd be so kind as to lend me your ear for a few minutes."

When you approach him in this nonthreatening, will-you-help-me kind of way, even the most withdrawn of kids isn't likely to say no. With your wording, you are saying that you respect him and his thinking, and you respect his opinion enough to ask for it. Most adults don't ask for opinions from kids. They lecture them as if they are two-year-olds on what they should do.

When you know you've got his attention, you say, "I can't stop thinking about Ryan. He must have been in so much pain to take his life. His death seems so senseless to me, and I don't know what to do with the feelings of sadness I have. I know you were really close to him. Could you maybe help me process my thoughts and feelings about this? I'm coming up blank, but I still feel depressed about it, even though it's been a couple of months now. Do you understand what happened?"

Such gentle conversation will put you and Andrew on the same "adult" playing field because you are inviting your son to help you. The fact is, Andrew has no answers for what happened either. He's as stupefied as you are. He's never seen a 15-year-old in a casket before. Before this, *suicide* was just a word to him—something he saw on the news. Then suddenly suicide became a real, close, personal experience.

Any conversation you have regarding the tragedy of suicide in general, therefore, is useless. It has to be personal. Worrying about your son who is sitting in the dark isn't useful either. Engaging him in conversation is.

Andrew may not be ready to talk at this time. If not, accept that. Tell him, "You may not have any answers either, and if that's the case, I understand. It helped to be able to share my sadness with you."

If he isn't talking in a few days or a week, you might want to revisit the conversation by saying, "You know, I was thinking about our conversation last Thursday. Thanks for listening to me. That was really important. As hard as talking about Ryan's suicide is, I honestly did feel better after talking to you. I know he was your friend, and I care what you think. Sharing my thoughts made me feel a little lighter."

That's a commercial announcement in your own home, saying, *Hey, things get better when we can talk about them and share the burden.* If you approach Andrew in such a way, he might bite on that and follow through with more discussion on his own timetable. With teenagers, timing for discussion is everything.

Note that you're not saying, "Hey, kid, you better start talking." Nor are you demanding, "I want to know. What do you think happened? How are you feeling about it? Have you ever felt like ending your life?" Peppering an adolescent with questions is the fastest way to shut him down.

If Andrew doesn't respond to several attempts of conversation—spaced over a couple of weeks—and continues withdrawing from life, it's time to seek the help of a professional.

There's something you need to know about anger. When it is turned inward, it can become dangerous and even deadly. Every person who takes their own life is angry. That anger, not dealt with, led to the ultimate revenge tactic—suicide. If you see anger in your own child and he's demonstrating it with things like smashing his guitar, that's a reason for concern. You need to pay attention. Boys and girls both attempt suicide, but boys are more likely to succeed in those attempts. That's because they often choose harsher, more violent means—ones there is no coming back from—whereas girls are more likely to swallow pills, which can be rectified if caught in time.

Have that conversation with your son today if possible. If he doesn't talk, try again in a few days. If that attempt doesn't work, seek professional counseling immediately. He won't like getting hauled into a shrink's office, but your doing so will show him, if nothing else, how concerned you are for his welfare. That's at least a starting place to address his grief.

Could She Be Depressed?

Q: Rachel's almost 18. She's always been artistic and expressive and has coped well with life. However, this past year her sweet temperament has become explosive. She swings from high to low frequently and cries five to six times a day. Sometimes she doesn't shower for days. She doesn't return calls from her friends. She only sits in her room. When I asked her why, she said, "Mom, I don't know why. I just feel sad."

Could she be depressed? Does she need depression medicine?

Other times she acts like she's high on a caffeine buzz and doesn't sleep for a couple of days.

What exactly is going on? Does she need medical help?

A: A high school senior crying every once in a while because she feels sad is a normal, healthy response. However, crying jags of five to six times a day is not. Frequent swings from high to low like you're describing aren't typical behavior either.

A visit to a gynecologist who deals with hormone imbalances would be a good start. Testing will show if she needs any assistance with hormone imbalances, since they could greatly affect her physical condition and emotional state. If more assistance is needed, the doctor can also make referrals to other trusted professionals, such as psychologists or psychiatrists, for further evaluation.

As a psychologist, I wasn't an MD, and thus I didn't prescribe medicine. I provided counseling. In select cases, I referred my patients to psychiatrists, who were MDs, or back to their family doctors. In most of those situations, I knew there was something off center about the clients who walked in. There was a lack of connection, a nonresponsive attitude, a lack of caring about life or anything that happened to them. Some of those kids needed antidepressants.

The kids I referred, though, were rare ones I knew needed more help than my counseling could give them. Those kids were usually older teens—seniors in high school or in their first couple of years of college. Typically, it wasn't the students themselves who called for the appointment. It was their parents who phoned and begged me to meet with the kid.

"Something's off," the parent would say. "When I ask her what she did after school, she says, 'Nothing.' She isn't sleeping well. She has a lot of mood swings. Could you meet with her?"

That's your role right now, parent. Your daughter needs you to be her advocate.

Most schools are well stocked with professionals who are skilled in dealing with such matters. Now is the time to consult them. Your daughter may not be happy you talked to someone else about her, but her well-being is at stake. Sometimes assistance is accepted more easily if it's from a third party. So talk to the professionals. Get some appointments set up with a gynecologist and a counselor. Let them help you with the next steps.

If there is an onset of mental illness in a child's life, frequently it will develop in the late teenage years—18, 19, even early 20s. That hits the college-age group. Why are these years the target?

So much about mental illness remains a mystery, but we do know that the onset of schizophrenia and manic depression starts about that time because of the psychological makeup and development of human beings. A kid can still be depressed before that time, but the more serious mental illnesses begin during those ages. The male brain, for example, isn't fully developed until about age 25.

The abrupt changes you're seeing in your daughter are a red flag. She needs help for whatever is going on, and in her state she's not likely to seek it out herself. She needs you to intervene. Her classes at school are not as important as her well-being.

Step up to the plate now. The stakes are high. Anything you go through for your daughter's sake is well worth it.

Sexting Scandal

Q: I'm furious, and my 16-year-old's really hurting. She did something admittedly stupid—snapped a picture of herself shirtless and sent it to her boyfriend, who'd asked for it. But then he group-texted it to his friends. I found out when a teacher spotted it and called me as the parent of the photo's originator.

I'm in shock. I can't believe she did that in the first place. And I'm angry that her boyfriend passed something so private to other parties. My daughter's so embarrassed she says she'll never go to school again. What to do?

A: No doubt your daughter is devastated, and rightfully so. She did something stupid, and now she's paying for it with a lot of embarrassment in a dog-eat-dog adolescent world.

What can you do? Well, you can't turn back time and change the situation. That picture, even if you demand its removal, is out there for all eternity on the web or in somebody's saved pics. Nor can you change the fact that her boyfriend is a hormone-laden boy who shared the picture to up his competitive edge with the male population.

So where do you start? It makes sense to start with your daughter, the originator of the act. If she hadn't taken the photo, it wouldn't be out there circulating, would it?

You might think what I'm going to say next is a bit cruel, but bear with me. After you've caught your breath and calmed your own anger, you need to have a candid conversation with your daughter. "In the past, you've always used good judgment. However, in this situation, I'm disappointed in your lack of judgment. How you thought that taking such a picture would be okay in the first place is beyond my reasoning. Even if your boyfriend asked for it, that doesn't mean you should give it to him."

Yes, your words will sting. Your daughter already knows you're disappointed in her, and kids hate for their parents to be disappointed in them. Tears will likely be flowing now if they weren't already, but buck up, parent. Nobody said parenting is easy. To protect that daughter of yours from future trauma, your words and actions in this case are critical. Your daughter has already learned a big lesson the tough way in today's social media–driven culture. Your job isn't to rub her nose in it but to bring a dash of reality that will impact what she does from now on.

You add, "I know that taking and sending that picture was probably a spur-of-the-moment thing. We've all done those stupid kinds of things. But some, like this one, have bigger consequences that you'll have to live with. We've tried to bring you up with values and morals. But I'm wondering at this point what your own values, morals, and guidelines are."

If she's like most kids, she hasn't really thought about adopting morals, values, and guidelines for herself, separate from the ones you've reared her with that linger in the back of her head. Likely she flies with the wind. Snapping the picture in the first place and then sending it are both examples of her following her feelings instead of thinking through the situation first. In today's dangerous world, now is the time to right the ship that's going in the wrong direction before it runs into an iceberg and sinks.

You can use this situation as a teachable moment to address the following topics:

- "What information is private and shouldn't be given out?" (For example, full name, social security number, schedule, phone, email, home address, school name.)
- "What is and what isn't okay to post on social media? There are perks and dangers to social media. Once a photo or statement is on the internet in any way, it can be accessed even years from now. It's not truly removable. That inappropriate picture could be accessed by the person looking at your college application or a résumé for your first job. In today's sue-happy society, it's critical to think before you text."
- "What are your standards in dating guys? What do you look for, think you should put up with, or not tolerate?"
- "What kind of sexual behavior is okay to engage in with guys? A lot of kids have sex on the first date. Do you think you really owe that to any guy?"

Then you also need to address her ever-present reality. It's easy to understand why she doesn't want to return to school. But again, in order for this life lesson to stick and make her think through her future decisions more carefully, state the facts kindly but firmly.

"I thoroughly understand why you don't want to go back to that school. If I were you, I wouldn't want to show my head around that place either. But honestly, there aren't a lot of other choices where we live. We can't afford the private school down the street. But you know what? You're a strong kid. You've shown evidence of that all throughout your life. Remember when . . . *[share a time your daughter stood strong when times were tough]*? Wow, that showed me you can overcome anything. So here's the deal. You'll continue in school there."

She'll likely start to protest.

You add, "But you and I are going to work on some ready-made answers that you can give when people say things to you. For example, if someone refers to that picture, you respond with your head held high. 'Wow, talk about being dumb. I was dumber than mud to do that. That'll never happen again, ever.' That's a positive statement that simply says, 'Lesson learned.' And life moves on. You don't act beaten down or embarrassed. You're smart enough not to let anyone get the best of you. If you admit you did something dumb, the kids who want to hold the picture over your head won't have any leverage to try to make you miserable. Hold out for a few days by doing that, and soon the posse will move on to some other unlucky victim."

By doing this, your daughter admits her mistake, rises above it, and becomes committed to acting differently in the future.

Now, what about that boyfriend? I can see the steam rising from your ears as I mention the kid. After this, it isn't likely the two are a pair anymore. A betrayal like that and the stars in your daughter's eyes have dimmed. (If not, you need another conversation about what she should put up with in a relationship and what to look for in a guy.) That boy needs to be dealt with in a meeting with the principal of the school and both sets of parents in the room. You don't need to press charges or cause any more ruckus—kids will do stupid things. But that boy needs to feel the sting of his actions so he doesn't do this again with another hapless girl.

You also need to make sure the photo is deleted from your daughter's phone and her boyfriend's phone. The problem is, if the boy had an inner circle of 20 guys always texting and it's a group thing, now 20 of his friends have the photo too. So do what you can through the school to track and insist that it be deleted from all their devices too.

The possibility remains that the photo may rear its head sometime in your daughter's future. Electronic pics travel at the speed of light—especially photos like that with adolescent boys. Most boys would fire it around like nobody's business, even download and make copies of it. So act quickly to quell any further distribution of the picture.

Then you have to calm down and let life return to normal. Believe it or not, it will. Hopefully your daughter is much wiser now about social media . . . and the maturity level of her next potential boyfriend.

She Hates Me and Wants to Live with Her Daddy

Q: I've just come out on the other side—finally—of a very messy divorce. My husband yelled a lot and made life intense for me and the kids. We all started showing signs of stress. For instance, one of my kids who had been potty trained for a year started wetting the bed again. When he slapped me once in the middle of a fight, I decided it was time to get out. My number one priority was to protect my kids and give them the best life possible, meaning their physical and emotional safety first.

According to the court, we share custody, but my ex decided he wanted the kids only in the summers. By the time the first summer came, he had a live-in girlfriend. He said she didn't want kids underfoot, so he took a pass. I was glad the kids could stay with me, in a more stable environment.

My three younger kids (now 3, 4, and 5) don't mention their daddy at all. I'm not even sure they remember him. But my 11-year-old will barely talk to me. She's very angry. She says that the divorce is all my fault and she hates me. She wants to go live with her daddy. That really hurts, and I don't understand it. Would you give me some perspective?

A: All parties involved in a divorce come out hurting—particularly the children. Dads are huge in a daughter's life, so it's no surprise she's saying what she is. She's suffering from "daddy hunger." Unlike the other kids, she remembers him being in your home. Because she longs for him to be home, she's likely built up a fairy-tale world in her mind. She remembers the good experiences—when her daddy threw her up in the air, caught her, and laughed with her, for example—and has built a make-believe world around that.

How good things would be, she thinks, *if Mom and Dad would get back together, and we'll all live happily ever after.*

You're the problem, she believes. You broke up with her dad. You could get him back if you wanted, but you won't try. It's all your fault.

Trying to combat your daughter's thinking won't get you anywhere. She'll merely work harder to turn that ex-husband of yours into the father of the year. Arguing that he does this and that won't make a dent in her determined psyche to get her father back into her life somehow. You also can't change the legal document that says he has a right to see his kids.

Your daughter might be throwing out "I hate you and I want to go live with Dad" as an anger management tool. She might also feel bad that Dad is by himself, with none of his original family, and that you have all four kids. She may be, in a strange but predictable way, trying to even things out. Or she may be using you and your ex against each other to gain sympathy or something she wants.

Regardless of her motives, right now it's impossible for your daughter psychologically to appreciate what you've gone through to keep your family intact. But you can at least initiate a conversation. A few fragments might stick for her to ruminate on.

"I know you've expressed a couple of times that you're displeased with me and that you want to live with your father. I know this divorce hasn't been easy on you, or any of us. However, the fact that you want to live with your dad concerns me for a couple of reasons. First, I've gone to a lot of time and effort to keep you and your siblings together, because I believe that's a good idea. Second, Dad's yelling can get out of control when he's stressed. That worries me because I don't want to see you treated that way."

Let me clarify an important point here, Mom. It's critical that you understand this before you decide on your next steps. Yelling every once in a while is different from being verbally abusive. We're all human. We get angry and upset sometimes. But occasionally losing our temper and yelling because we're stressed is far different from a pattern of denigrating others with words. Those who abuse in such a way feel bad about themselves, so they put others down to try to make themselves feel better. It's a vicious cycle that injures both parties.

If your ex is verbally abusive, you can never allow your 11-year-old to make the decision of where she wants to live. Your answer is firm. "Living with your dad full-time is not an option. However, if you want to see him, you can give him a call and arrange a time to get together." If he reneged on the summer option and has a new girlfriend, he may not even find a time to get together. Your problem is solved without you having to utter a word.

But if your ex simply loses his temper at times and does life differently from you, give your daughter the opportunity to live with him. "If you truly want to live with your dad, give him a call and tell him that. See what he says. If he agrees, then you would go to live there for a year. At the end of that year, you'd have the chance to change that option. But you couldn't go for a few weeks or a month and then come back home. If you go, you'd stay there for an entire school year."

The worst thing for middle schoolers is to bounce back and forth from home to home like a Ping-Pong ball served from one court to the other. They need consistency, and they won't get that when they spend most of their time in the air between locations. She also needs to know, at age 11, that her decisions matter. Just because she changes her mind doesn't mean others will adapt to what she wants. Otherwise, you'll create a teenager who thinks she can wave her pinkie willy-nilly and get others to cater to her every wish.

Let's say she does call her dad. With his track record, he's likely to stammer out a shocked "I'll think about it" and put off the decision, hoping she'll change her mind. When he ends up saying no, she'll be crushed and hurting, but it's not your fault that her dad rejected her. Reality did the talking and straightened out her thinking. Now she needs a good dose of mommy love in the form of a hug.

You, Mom, are her stable home. In this situation, you need to be patient. Let time pass, and your daughter will probably see her dad's true colors—or she may not. Even if you are the mother of the year, she may defend her father for all sorts of reasons. She might feel sorry for him, believe he's the weaker parent, or worry that he's lonely. He may have been a terrible father and husband, but he's still your daughter's father. You can't control what he does or what happens in his home, but you can have a significant influence over what happens in your own.

Caught Cheating

Q: My oldest son was caught cheating on a big exam a couple of weeks ago. His private high school is very picky about things like that, so they immediately suspended him. It got worse when they found out a group of students were involved. They issued an ultimatum to Carter: "Tell us who else is involved and we'll discipline but not expel you. Don't tell us and we'll expel you."

We're in shock. Why would our straight-A student cheat and be part of an organized cheating scheme? Even more, he's refusing to say who else is involved or who started it. We're stupefied. Why would he put group loyalty to a bunch of high schoolers over potentially getting expelled? I know he's hurting and embarrassed, but his decision right now can make the difference in his college options.

We know what we would do, but how can we force him to make the right decision if he won't talk? Worse, it happened near the end of his junior year, when he was starting to think about what colleges to apply to. There's a month left of school. Should we try to stall the administration until it's summer, to see if they'll change their mind or if our son will decide to tell who's involved?

A: First of all, you can't force any kid to talk who doesn't want to talk, so give up that notion right now. In fact, the more you try to encourage your son to talk, the tighter he'll clamp his mouth shut merely to spite you. Also, his private high school is right to be "picky" about cheating. Cheating is rampant in schools. Better to learn the lesson about honesty and integrity earlier in life than later. Good for the school for holding their students to high standards.

Let me ask you a question: whose problem is this really—yours or your son's? Sure, you're embarrassed. But who is the sole individual who will be most impacted by this in the future? Your son. If you continue to try to solve this problem for him, he won't learn anything, and worse things will happen in the future because he got off scot-free.

Carter is about to learn a huge lesson in life . . . the hard way. Noble as it sounds not to be the high school narc, he is making a grievous mistake. Other kids who cheated with him will go off to the colleges of their choice and do what they want to do. He won't be able to do that, because he'll get expelled. A switch in schools and the reason for it will show up on his permanent records, which all college administrators see. You think a football team would want to scout him then? A med school? A business university?

Your son is trading what he thinks is popularity—very fleeting in high school circles—for his future.

What should you do? Lay low. If he won't talk, you can't help him. Let the realities of the situation do the talking through natural consequences:

1. If he doesn't talk, he gets expelled.
2. He'll have to make up the last month of course work in summer school somewhere.
3. In the fall, he'll have to transfer to another high school for his senior year, and his record that he was academically disqualified for cheating will follow him.
4. That record will be sent to any colleges or universities he applies to and will garner a lot of rejections. His pool to pick from might be amazingly slim . . . or nonexistent.

Carter might initially think that getting the last month of school off isn't too bad. However, he'll whistle a different tune when he finds out he'll have to make up the course work elsewhere, and it'll likely take him a lot longer. Even more so when you say, "Well, since school isn't a part of the equation now, we expect you to get a job for this month and through the summer. So what's your game plan?"

When he talks about colleges he's going to apply to, you reply, "Well, good luck with that," and go about your business.

Parent, if you don't keep the ball in your son's court now, you'll make a fatal mistake. You'll teach him that his actions don't matter because you'll always rescue him. Instead, he needs to feel the pain of his error in judgment. One mistake doesn't mean life has ended, but it can certainly change the ball game.

That straight-A son of yours may end up working a job for a year or two and find out how tough earning a living really is, or he may go to a community college for a couple of years and have to work hard to dispel his cheating background so he can get accepted by a university.

If you let reality do the talking, you don't have to lecture. Your blood pressure doesn't rise. You don't have to become the bad guy or gal to your son. Your home doesn't become a war zone. And Carter learns through natural consequences how important honesty and integrity really are.

Before I sign off on this topic, I don't want to miss addressing a critical element. Just *why* did your straight-A son cheat in the first place? Is it because he couldn't say no to peer pressure? Because being part of a certain group was more important than the basic values you taught him at home? It's likely that was a factor. If so, he's a normal adolescent. Or was it because he was afraid of failing? That he feared he couldn't meet your expectations on that particular test?

Firstborns are perfectionists, with high expectations of themselves. They also feel the heavy mantle of family expectations—your son was your guinea pig in parenting, so you heaped more pressures on him as a result. If you don't believe that, think for a minute what your baby of the family gets away with as compared to your firstborn. Enough said?

Firstborns naturally feel the sting of parental criticism the most because they are primed to succeed. That means they also experience a deep worry of failure. Carter may have cheated because he feared failure . . . and subsequently disappointing you. If either of you, Mom or Dad, tends to criticize him, it's time to confront your own high expectations with a reality check, especially now that the situation has changed. You may not like what your son has done, and it's not your role to rescue him, but he still needs to feel your unconditional love and support. Part of that is having a frank conversation at a timely moment regarding *why* he chose to cheat.

Before you do that, take a realistic look in the mirror at your responses to your son. Are you over-the-top in your parental expectations? If so, now is the time to admit that to him and work together on solutions.

Grieving Stepchild

Q: This is a first marriage for me, but a second for my husband. His first wife, a good friend of mine, passed away when Jessi was 10 and Corey was 4. I feel very fortunate to have been first their beloved "auntie" who spent a lot of time with them, and now, two years later, their new "mom."

The kids and I have always had a good relationship, but I can feel Jessi pulling away from me a bit since Jeff and I got married. I can't quite put a finger on how our relationship changed, but I'm guessing it might be because now I'm in a mom role instead of the auntie she could laugh with and have fun with.

She's still a really sweet girl, kind to me, and protective of her little brother. But I've heard her cry a couple of times in her room, peeked in, and seen her holding her mom's photo. I never know whether to try to comfort her or leave her alone. I can never replace my friend or the mom she loves, but I want to be there for her.

When she's grieving, how can I help? I miss my special friend too.

A: Kudos to you, because you already understand you can't replace Jessi's mom. Even better, you knew well and loved the person she also misses. The fact that Jessi is still sweet and kind to you shows that the two of you have a good, solid relationship invested in years of trust. You merely need to get over this little road bump. And due to the nature of grief, don't be surprised if you hit a few more of these bumps.

When someone dies, loved ones often cope with their grief by not talking about the deceased person for fear of making someone in the family cry. But crying is really okay. Bottling up that sadness is not, for either of you. Sharing memories—sad ones, happy ones, goofy ones—is critically important to healing.

The next time Jessi is crying in her bedroom, I'd do this. Gently knock on the door and say, "Hey, may I come in for a minute?" Then sit on the edge of her bed, put your arm around her, and state the obvious. "You miss your mom, don't you? Wow, we all miss her."

At this point, Jessi will probably break down and cry. Hold that girl tighter. "Oh, Jessi, if you need to cry, that's fine. I know you miss your mom. She knows you miss her." Make that very important connection for a child. Then add, "I'm glad you love looking at her photos. I do too." Point at the photo and say, "I remember when she . . ." Share a sweet memory of your departed friend, how much she meant to you, and how much she loved her kids.

"I find myself in tears sometimes too, missing her," you tell Jessi. "So can we cut a deal? The next time you're sad and you feel like you want somebody with you, come and get me and take my hand. Ditto when I need you. We can talk about anything you want to. We can remember your mom together. Does that sound okay to you?"

By responding in such a way, you are inviting her to grieve with you and to tell stories that may make you both cry but can lead to laughter and a closer bond. You also aren't ignoring the elephant in the room and tiptoeing around it.

"Being honest and real is extremely important," Lisa Beamer told me when we met at a shared publicity event. As the widow of 9/11 hero Todd Beamer, she had two young children and a baby on the way when she received the news of her husband's death. "I didn't want them to forget their daddy or how much he loved them." Because her children were so young, she went out of her way to keep family photos scattered around the house at the children's eye level. She wanted the kids to pick them up and look at their daddy.

Keeping photos scattered around the house of the kids with their mom and of you with your friend is a great idea. Pick them up every once in a while, smile, and tell a story. "I remember when this photo was taken. We were . . ."

Grief shared together truly is much lighter.

Sexual Abuse in the Family

Q: I was devastated recently to find out that my brother-in-law sexually abused my 8-year-old daughter when she was at his house on a sleepover with her cousin (who I just discovered has also been sexually abused by him). My sister knew her second husband "had a problem" but covered it up, thinking it was "only" a one-time thing. She says she didn't want to ruin her second marriage—or her financial income—because of a single incident. I don't want to ruin my sister's life, but the safety of my child comes first.

I'm vitriolically angry—no other way to say it—that my innocent daughter had to experience such trauma in a place we thought was safe. She has become very fearful and cries a lot. She woke up screaming last night. We rushed in and found her cowering under the covers, hugging her knees.

Because it's family, how do we handle this situation? My husband is very protective and wants to pursue it legally, as well as cut off all relationships with my sister and brother-in-law. No way do we want our daughter to have contact with him ever again, but what's the right thing to do?

A: Sadly, most sexual abuse happens within the family—the place where children should be loved and protected most. Let me be clear. It's a *crime*, not a one-time event. Don't even think of deferring to your sister, who has her own issues for allowing such aberrant behavior to go on under her roof and then excusing it.

Your husband is right. You have to be hard and strong and go the legal route. That means contacting the police and also cutting that man off from any physical contact with your child. By taking those steps, you're making a statement to your daughter that you believe her and back her, and that her safety is most important.

Nothing is worse than child abuse, in my view. Parents should take all the legal action they can, even if the perpetrator is a family member. Your daughter is only 8. She's already showing psychological signs that she's been deeply wounded by the trauma. She needs to talk about what happened not only with you, Mom and Dad, but with a trusted professional who can walk all of you through the stages of recovery. She will need support now and down the road in adolescence, when she starts developing physically.

It's important to meet with a professional who is skilled in dealing with children who are sexually abused. There are many different types of sexual abuse, which need to be addressed accordingly. Sexual abuse can range from inappropriate touching to forcing a kid to have oral sex to actual penetration. At her age, your daughter may not even know how to describe exactly what happened to her, or she may choose to block it out.

You've married a smart man, so back him in all his actions to take the perpetrator to court. If you stick your head in the sand because of your sister, you're doing her and everyone in your family—including that little cousin—a terrible disservice. Your sister needs psychological counseling as well.

This situation might ruin your relationship as sisters. But it also forces her to accept the reality of what's been going on in her home and address the personal issues that allow her to excuse this type of behavior, and it provides the opportunity to protect her own child in the future.

Because there is a high probability that sexual abusers will be within the family—a parent, grandparent, uncle, aunt, or cousin—it's wise to teach even very young children that private areas of their body are to be kept private and not be touched by anybody except a doctor on a doctor's visit. An easy way that makes sense even to the youngest kids is establishing the sacredness of the "swimsuit line." It's a simple formula: nobody should touch anything that should be covered by a swimsuit.

Stick to your guns on this one. I know it's going to be tough, especially because other family members may not understand and think you're being too hard on your sister's husband. But your parental priority is providing security for your daughter. Family gatherings can go on without you if you're ostracized for doing what's right. Those are small sacrifices in light of the trust you're building with your daughter that will last for her lifetime.

MIA Ex

Q: I hate seeing the disappointed look on my son's face every time my ex doesn't show up for an event. He wants to sit outside our apartment door, waiting for his daddy. Last time he sat there for two hours with his baseball glove for Mr. No-Show. It broke my heart.

It's hard enough on the kid that our family broke up and we had to move out of our house and neighborhood, but my ex is making it worse. I've run out of excuses for his irresponsible behavior. Callum is only 7, but I know he feels rejected by his daddy.

Our court agreement insists my ex has visiting rights, but he rarely follows through on his promises. I can't make him show up. So what can I say and do to heal the hurt in my son's heart? I can't become his father too.

A: You're right. You can't make your ex show up. It's time to stop making excuses for the guy who isn't dependable. When your son is sitting there with that baseball glove in hand and your ex doesn't show, likely the tears will roll. Or, if it's happened enough, your son might get angry.

When Callum asks, "Where is he, Mom? Why isn't he coming?" don't offer any excuses. Don't say, "Well, maybe something came up." If you do, you're merely enabling your ex's bad behavior. Instead, be honest but without venom (which is particularly tough when you see how much your child is hurting). An honest answer would be, "I have no idea. Why don't you give him a call and find out?"

Don't *you* make the call. After all, you're the ex. Have your son call. Your ex hearing your son's crying or being on the receiving end of his anger may accomplish what you never could—a healthy dose of guilt. Plus your ex will have to explain to Callum why he's not there. Lame excuses won't hold up with a 7-year-old.

If your son can't reach your ex, then say, "Well, next time you see him you can certainly ask him."

Then changing the environment will help. "Since he's not here, why don't you and I do something else?" Touch your son's shoulder or reach for his hand. "How about we . . . *[make a suggestion]*? Or do you have another idea of something fun you'd like to do? I'm all ears."

You might play Frisbee at a local park or bake chocolate-chip cookies together (it's okay if they're from a tube in your refrigerator—you don't have to be a master baker to produce tantalizing aromas in your kitchen). Just do something you know Callum would enjoy.

In other words, turn the tables on the negative experience. Don't give in to your temptation to bad-mouth your ex. If you talk bad about his daddy, your son will turn him into the father of the year in his imagination. It's just the way the psyche works of kids in divorced-family situations.

Your son will figure out for himself that your ex isn't dependable, but he can count on you. Rising to the situation and prompting a positive memory that you two can share helps to cement your closeness as mother and son. Callum may not be able to count on his dad, but Mom is there, rock-solid and not moving in his life. That kind of knowledge creates security in a world that he thought originally was safe but turned topsy-turvy with your divorce.

You're also right that you can't be his father. You shouldn't try to be. You can't replace his daddy in his life. Your son will resent you for trying, and it'll be awkward for both of you. So don't be the one who tries to play baseball with him—what his daddy would normally do. Instead, find positive role models—your brother, your father, a close family friend—who can do "guy" things with your son. Also, show respect for him being a boy. Ask for his help every once in a while, and you'll watch his miniscule muscles flex with male pride.

But what Callum needs most from you right now is for you to be exactly what you are—his mother. Focus your energy on that, and strive to be the most consistent, loving, and communicative mom you can be. If you do, you'll have a son who loves his mama even when he's grown up and out of the nest.

Pregnant at 15

Q: I never thought it would be us in this situation. But Shelli, our 15-year-old, is pregnant. My husband and I are so shocked, we don't know what to do next. We didn't know until her morning sickness hit full throttle and she couldn't hide it any longer.

She's been dating a 17-year-old guy—they're both in high school—since the beginning of the school year. He's a nice guy, and we know his parents too. They're good people who go to the same church we do. That's why we allowed the kids to date, even though Shelli isn't 16 yet, and being that age was our family's rule. We had no idea they were sexually involved.

But a baby? Those kids aren't ready for a baby. They can't take care of a baby, and they're certainly not ready to get married.

Abortion isn't an option because of our beliefs. But we also thought that college, a career, and marriage would be in Shelli's future before a kid hit the picture. What do we do now?

A: I understand you have very firm convictions of how things *should* go. For this situation to work out for your daughter, though, *she* has to be the person who makes that decision. After all, she is the one carrying that baby. I realize the two kids are 15 and 17, not ready to be parents. But they also were "adult" enough to get in that situation in the first place, so with that action, they moved beyond childhood.

That baby is not going away, so an important decision has to be made. It's critically important for your future relationship that what happens next is your *daughter's* decision. Although she is your child, she is the mother of that baby.

You said you had dating rules—not dating until age 16, for example. That's older than many kids start dating today. You also said you allowed the two kids to date because they went to the same church. (By the way, just because kids go to church doesn't mean that they have reduced hormone levels or urges.) So Shelli is used to a rule-oriented household and Mom or Dad making decisions for her. But don't mistake that for meaning she always agrees with those decisions or holds the same values as you. She is sorting all that out for herself as she becomes an adult.

In this situation, most parents—especially authoritarian ones—will decide the game plan. They'll say, "Okay, this is what we're going to do. You know we don't believe in abortion. So we'll send you to Aunt Cassie's in Michigan before you start showing. You can stay there and be homeschooled while you have the baby. We'll tell the school and everybody else that since you miss your aunt and want to spend time with her, you'll be there for the next year. It's perfect timing since the baby will be born in June. You can recuperate there for the summer and then go back to your school here in the fall like nothing happened. And Aunt Cassie has some contacts there to help set up a private adoption."

But you shouldn't do that. Your daughter will resent you for the rest of her life. Your role right now should be simply to facilitate a discussion. "Since we all know each other, let's get everybody in the same room so we can talk."

You set up the meeting with the other parents. Meet on neutral turf if possible. Then introduce the topic. "Okay, we're here to talk. Shelli, what are your thoughts and feelings? How would you like to handle this?"

Give her time to talk without interrupting. Then ask the young man the same thing and give him time to talk without interrupting. You'll swiftly know whether the young couple is on the same page or not, and also whether their thoughts are realistic or not.

If you develop a warm, inviting environment in which your daughter and her boyfriend can talk, you'll have an opening to hopefully guide the kids toward making the right decision.

Aborting a child can do long-term physical damage, which can lessen your daughter's chances of having a baby later in life. There's also a significant emotional and psychological impact. Choosing abortion can thrust her into a sense of deep loss and guilt. She may struggle with regret, depression, or suicidal thoughts, to name a few post-traumatic consequences. Abortion might seem like an "easy fix"—to rescue you all from embarrassment and make the "problem" go away—but the consequences of that action are life-long for the female who carried the baby.

But let me emphasize something else I feel strongly about. There is an important third party involved—the child. The emphasis has to remain on what's best for the child, which is—hands down in this situation—placing the child for adoption.

A 15-year-old and a 17-year-old are not ready to raise a baby together. You, as grandparents, may not want to be thrust into the position of being surrogate parents for the baby while your daughter finishes high school. However, sometimes a family follows that plan because they don't want to lose a child who is of their bloodline.

The young couple also should not be pressured to marry just because a baby is in the picture. Young couples who do marry due to parental pressure often don't stay together past the birth of the baby.

However, your daughter has the opportunity to place this child in the arms of two parents who are longing for and anticipating the arrival of a child in their home. They're waiting for a miracle.

I myself know the miracle of adoption through watching the shining eyes of my daughter Hannah and son-in-law Josh, who adopted twins. My own tears overflowed at seeing those precious babies in the hands of their overjoyed new mama and papa. I will be forever grateful for the gift of that birth mom.

When you're overwhelmed by the situation, look at it from that angle—that a new life has been created. You are now partners with your daughter in watching over that little life in its early stages. If your daughter chooses an open adoption, she will have the opportunity to be a part of that baby's life and his or her new family. In that case, your family will simply grow larger, with room for more love.

Too Sensitive?

Q: Daniel, who's 9, has always been sensitive. He gets very attached to the people and things he loves. He likes predictable things and doesn't deal well with change.

A year ago he cried for a week when his pet goldfish died. We finally bought him two new goldfish, thinking that would help heal the hurt. A couple months ago, our family dog had to go to the vet after being hit by a car. A neighbor had to take the dog because Daniel was so upset that I had to stay home with him. Those same neighbors could have watched Daniel for me, but he was inconsolable. It took me sitting beside him to watch a favorite movie, complete with an ice cream treat, to calm him down. Meanwhile, I was worried about the dog the whole time.

Two weeks ago, Daniel's uncle, whom he's very close to (my husband's brother), was diagnosed with cancer. Sadly, it's in a progressed state, and things aren't looking good. Do we tell Daniel or not? What if he can't handle it?

A: Lots of things happen in life that aren't planned and aren't fun, like goldfish dying, dogs getting hit by cars, and loved ones being diagnosed with cancer. Cushioning your child from tragedy and sadness might seem like a good move to calm the immediate storm, but it won't help your son stand on his own feet when you're not around.

Let me do some guessing here. I could be wrong, but a lot of times my guesses are spot-on. Daniel is probably an only child or the oldest child in your family, right? I believe you've become *too good* of a parent. Yes, you read that right. You've paid too much attention to your "sensitive" son.

Every time I hear the word *sensitive*, I translate that as something else—a powerful child who is growing more and more skilled at manipulating you. In your own words, you said you "had to" stay home with Daniel when the dog was hit by a car. You didn't have to, but you chose to, because you know well the fallout that's already there or soon going to be there if you go against Daniel's wishes.

Your son has faced a couple of hits, but nothing unusual for childhood. In fact, I've always told parents that goldfish are great first pets. They have a short life span, so you won't have to take care of them when your child goes off to college. Also, there's direct cause and effect to teach responsibility: you have to feed the goldfish for it to survive.

Every kid cries and gets sad when hard things happen. Daniel might have forgotten to feed the goldfish, or its life span was over. Either way, the result is the same—a belly-up fish. Daniel got an up-close view of what death is like when his goldfish didn't come back.

But Daniel's response to the goldfish's death was an overreaction. Crying for a week? That's over the top. Bluntly, he was workin' ya to get a couple of new goldfish, and you fell for it. You went out and bought them to cheer him up and curtail the constant noise in your home. So for a short stint, Daniel actually won double what he had before: two goldfish instead of one. In his young mind, that kid's mantra was, *I am the center of the universe. If I fuss enough and hold out, I'll get exactly what I want.*

Since his behavior worked to control you, he ramped it up when the dog was hit. Even though that dog needed you in his crisis, your son didn't want you to leave his sight. Yes, he was probably sad and scared. But such a time would have been a good learning experience.

The best solution would have been for you to hug him and say, "Daniel, I know you're scared that Buddy is hurt. You wonder what will happen to him. I feel that way too. But I need to leave now and take him to the vet. He needs someone with him. Mrs. Allen will stay with you while I'm gone."

And then off you go to take that dog, who is in intense pain, to the vet. This was your game plan: You conversed briefly with him to convey that you know he's scared, and you feel the same way. Then you told him the plan of action—important to first-borns and only children. Next you acted on that plan and weren't swayed by his pleading or tears. Such a game plan shows your child that he's important but the universe doesn't revolve around him. Responding in such a way to that incident would also have prepared him more effectively for this new and larger challenge—his uncle's cancer.

What should you do now? Tell Daniel about the situation. "Remember when Buddy got hurt by the car? He had to go to the vet and stay there for a while so he'd get better?"

Daniel nods.

"Well, Uncle Troy isn't feeling well right now. He has a sickness called cancer, and he's going to have to go to the hospital for a while."

Daniel's eyes widen and fill with tears. You feel the over-the-top reaction coming. Simply put your hand on his shoulder and say, "I know you feel sad. If you want to cry, it's okay."

Children don't need to know every blow by blow of a medical plan or the details as the cancer progresses. But they do need a dose of reality without the sugarcoating.

When Daniel asks, as he likely will, "Will Uncle Troy die like my goldfish?" you answer plainly, "That's possible, because he is very sick. But the doctors are doing all they can to help your uncle."

Isn't it cruel to tell an 8-year-old his uncle might die? you might be thinking.

It's the truth, though, and you shouldn't sugarcoat it. Creating a fantasyland where nobody dies is even more cruel in the long run. Your child will hate you for lying to him. Instead, this situation can be a teachable moment: everything that lives will also die at some point. Like the goldfish.

But then you move on. "What's most important right now is that we think of what's best for Uncle Troy, who is hurting. He needs our hugs and our love."

With these words, you've turned the attention from your son's feelings to the uncle who is in pain. This step is strategic because your son, who is used to being the center of the universe, needs to discover that other people matter too. Giving, rather than always receiving, is important. Doing something proactive will kick off that transition in your son's head.

"I bet Uncle Troy would love it if you drew him a picture," you say. "Today he's busy with tests at the hospital, but we could take it to him tomorrow. Maybe you and I could make his favorite dessert too."

Through this type of conversation, you've accomplished the following:

- informed Daniel that his uncle is ill
- admitted that the illness is serious
- acknowledged that the news might make Daniel sad, and that it's okay to cry
- stated that the focus needs to turn to the person who is hurting more—Uncle Troy
- told Daniel that he can do something active to be kind at a tough time for his uncle

This world, frankly, needs more givers and less takers, and it would indeed be a better place. Setting such priorities, even in a time of sadness, is very important to not only your child's well-being but also the well-being of those around him in the future.

At any time during the conversation, Daniel is likely to test you, so be forewarned. Sometimes sensitivity is manipulation. If his usual behavior crops up, say calmly, "I can see you're upset, so now is not a good time to finish the conversation. We'll talk more about it later."

Then turn your back and walk away. Go into a room or somewhere he can't follow you. As hard as it is, wait for his storm to subside. Since it's worked before, he'll give the test his all. You'll hear things you've probably never heard before.

But you're not being mean. You're being firm. If you give in now, you only create a more manipulative child, who thinks, *Ah, I see. If I keep it up for five minutes, she'll give in.*

If your child wants to have a meltdown, let him. Don't even try to stop him. But you disengage. If you don't give him an audience, it's amazing how swiftly the manipulation will end.

Sad things happen in life. Death is a part of life. But even these types of situations can be teachable moments that will develop your child into the resilient adult you want him to be someday.

Encounter with Racial Prejudice

Q: We're a biracial family. Because of my husband's job, we recently moved into an area that we soon discovered isn't very friendly to those they consider "different." My kids—7, 8, and 13—have faced some unkind comments.

After several months, the two youngest started to settle in and now seem to have adjusted okay to their new surroundings. The town kids have gotten used to them looking different, so they don't pick on them as much anymore. I think it helps that my younger boys are bigger than the average 7- and 8-year-old and hold their own on the playground.

But my once kind, well-adjusted 13-year-old seems to have morphed into a different person. At home he kicks doors and walls and argues. He picks fights a lot. Yesterday he ended up in the principal's office for punching another boy in the gut. When I asked him why he did that, he shook his head and said, "Whatever." He refused to say anything else, just went into his room and spent the night gaming. He didn't even show up at the dinner table.

We can't go on like this. Because we live in a smaller town and there's only one high school, there isn't a possibility of moving my oldest son to a different school. My husband's job will keep us in this area for two years. None of us can handle two years like this.

Ideas?

A: Every 13-year-old adolescent boy has a lot to sort through. That includes hormones, a rapidly changing body, and the drive to compete with other boys to be top dog. On top of that, your son has been catapulted out of the world he knows into a brand-new environment. In a small town especially, he's competing as a lone wolf among a group of individuals who have likely been together since babyhood. He's the new kid on the block trying to break in. That's never easy. Middle school can be particularly vicious as boys jockey for position with each other and try to get the attention of other species—aka, girls.

Not only that, he looks different from the other kids. In the middle school environment, "different" is an open invitation: "Go ahead, pick on me." That's exactly what's happening.

Your son is understandably frustrated. He also likely resents you as his parents for thrusting him into this place where he doesn't want to be. He needs a way to vent the feelings he obviously has about life. At home, he's kicking the walls and arguing with you. At school, he's picking fights to flex his muscles. It's the only way he knows how to say, "Hey, stop messing with me."

However, punching someone isn't a good way to handle that frustration. Physical violence isn't the answer and won't improve his reputation in the long term (though it might induce a little fear in those classmates so they'll think before they pick on him). Kicking the walls and doors and hitting people has to stop—now. So does the arguing with you.

What does your son need most? Your love and understanding at this tough time. He also needs some downtime in a calm space where he won't be judged or picked on. That's why he's retreating to his bedroom. He doesn't want you to ask how his day went, since it went just like all the others thus far—with him feeling ostracized for being biracial. He needs your home to be a safe environment where he doesn't have to be on guard, where he is loved unconditionally. But that doesn't mean you'll put up with nonsense, back talk, or bad behavior.

Getting on his case about punching the kid at school isn't the place to start. First, have an honest conversation.

"That was a rough day yesterday, huh? Getting hauled into the principal's office isn't any fun. I didn't like the call I got either. But you want to know something?" You look him in the eyes. "I know you. That's not you. You're a great kid, and you usually handle any trouble really well. So something's going on that's causing you to act that way. I'd like to do what I can, but having some details about what happened before you punched the kid would help. Did he say or do anything that upset you?"

In those few words, you definitely have your kid's attention. His ears are open. *Wow*, he's thinking, *Mom didn't hammer me for hitting that jerk. She's not yelling now either, or blaming me for what I did.*

His heart opens too, because you've basically said you believe in him and that he's capable of handling anything. *She thinks I'm usually a great kid. She even wants my side of the story.*

Sometimes adolescents are loyal and don't want to say what happened within the peer group. But in this case, your son is new enough to the group and doesn't have friends. He's likely to spill everything that went on.

When you hear the details, stay calm. They likely won't be pretty. People can get nasty when it comes to racial prejudice. However, you will get the ammunition you need to arrange a meeting between you, your son, and the principal. If that principal is a good, smart one, he'll arrange a meeting with the three of you, the offending students, and their parents, where everything can be aired in a professional setting.

Some apologies need to happen, because racial prejudice hits hard. You may not be able to change the mind-set of some of the students (or, frankly, their parents, which is where prejudicial views come from in the first place), but they need to come out into the light of day, where they look ugly and embarrassing.

Your son isn't off the hook either. He needs to apologize to the kid he socked. He must look that kid straight in the eyes and say,

"What I did was wrong. I never should have hit you. But the words you said really hurt me down deep. I'm new here, and I'm trying my best to fit in. Comments like that make me feel worthless and angry. That's why I hit you."

The principal should then take over, saying, "In our school, nobody gets put down" and "Comments like that are never acceptable." If he doesn't, and he takes the side of the other parents, you and your husband need to seriously consider moving somewhere else. None of your kids will fare well in that environment.

If you take such a stance, it's likely that there's one kid in that room who will feel some guilt and end up becoming a friend of your son's. If you want to give that possibility a nudge, here's a secret you need to know: middle school boys are always hungry. If you dangle a food option in front of your son and a potential friend, they'll go for it and gain a natural connection in the process.

For example, pick your son up after school armed with a couple of extra-large pizzas. I guarantee the aroma will get other boys' attention. There's nothing like an impromptu picnic on school grounds to ease the tension and launch potential friendships.

If your son mentions a particular boy, say, "Hey, if you ever want to invite Darren over after school, that's great with me. I'd be happy to pick you both up and then run him home later."

As for kicking walls and doors at your house, your son needs to know that isn't acceptable, even if he is frustrated. It'd be a good idea for him to clean off those scuff marks. Some boys need an active outlet for their growing testosterone.

One family I know was doing a big landscape project in their backyard. Their son would go out there and dig trenches and holes to let off steam after school. Sure, their yard was a mess for a couple of years, but their kid wasn't—and that was their priority. Whenever his parents saw a new large hole outside, they'd know Jake needed to talk. Jake and his dad spent a lot of time leaning on their shovels and talking through issues.

That was 10 years ago. The yard is now beautifully landscaped, thanks to Jake and his dad. Jake is 23, married, and living in another state, but not a week goes by that he and his parents don't talk heart-to-heart. The hours spent around the holes and the support his parents gave him at a rough time in middle school were truly an investment for the future.

Ditto for the time you're spending with your son and the effort you're making now.

Instagram Whiplash

Q: My daughter Amy has always been . . . well . . . a drama queen. That's a nice way to put it. Anything that happens—good or bad—puts her over the top. Ever since she turned 13, her mood swings could give you whiplash.

She also changes friends frequently. I sometimes wonder if it's because other kids get tired of her. To be honest, at times I do. Is that horrible to say about your own daughter?

When she loses a friend, she still doesn't learn that not everybody can tolerate her behavior. Yesterday her old best friend posted unflattering pictures of Amy in full drama queen mode on Instagram. Now texts on group chat are flying back and forth about the pics.

I know how cruel girls can be—I was a victim of that in school myself—so I want to protect her. Part of me knows she deserves a bit of what she got. The other part of me can't stand watching her cry. What exactly should I do in this situation?

A: I know you hate to see your daughter hurting, especially because you were picked on in school yourself. But in this situation, the best thing you can do is nothing. *Absolutely nothing.*

Here's what I mean. Right now your mama bear instincts are telling you to leap to your daughter's defense. However, you need to let reality do the teaching instead of you. The plain truth is that what your daughter sows, she'll reap. It's an ancient maxim and, honestly, the only way she'll learn to change her behavior. There's nothing like peer pressure and embarrassment—as much as you hate to see it happening—to change intolerable or stupid behavior in an adolescent. It works far faster than any parental lecture ever could.

At present she's looking for a little sympathy, but that won't help her in the long run. Some straight talk will.

"Kids can be nasty, huh?" you say to acknowledge the situation. "What's happened to you isn't very nice."

Her ears perk up at this. *Ah*, she's thinking, *here it comes—Mom to my defense.*

Instead you say, "You know I love you more than life itself. But I have to be honest with you. What happened could have been far worse, because your drama queen act is sometimes way over the top. Do you think some of your friends may be getting tired of your shenanigans, like Anna? And maybe that's why she did what she did?"

Then you plant an important thought to see if it'll germinate. "It's not easy to fit in and have people like you, especially at this age. One day they like you, and the next day they're ragging on you or posting pics that will embarrass you. Now, I'm just your mother, old as the hills, but here's a bit of advice. Lay low. Settle down before you say or do anything. If somebody mentions that picture, don't be quick to respond. Instead, take a breath and count to 10 before you open your mouth. During that time, think, *Would I want to see what I'm going to do next on Instagram?*"

If she's still in listening mode, add, "You can't go back and change what happened, but you can be smarter next time. If you say anything snarky back, you'll only incur more teasing and revenge tactics. Better to be calm about it all. When someone looks at you and snickers, look them straight in the eyes. Hanging your head will make them want to go after you more, since kids pick on the weakest person. If someone makes a comment about the picture, simply shrug and say, 'Yeah, that's me. I can be a drama queen sometimes. Lesson learned.' And then off you go to your next class. That will befuddle them because they've lost the edge they thought they had."

There's a term called *rabbit ears* that describes people who respond to everything. When rabbits are paying attention, focusing on something, their ears stand straight up. Let's say someone is ragging on the third baseman at the Little League game, calling out, "Hey, nice socks, buddy! Pull them up. Look like a real ballplayer, won't you?" He's trying hard to get the third baseman fluffed so he'll miss the catch. If the baseman responds by paying attention to that person, he's got rabbit ears.

If your daughter is known to have rabbit ears, she'll be easy pickings for her peer group. Becoming the calm bunny of the bunch has definite advantages. Yes, her personality might have a flair for drama. But controlling when and how she is dramatic—it's a good thing for the school play but not for a bad hair day—is an important skill to learn.

No parent wants their kid to get picked on. But going after the kids who posted her crazy moment on Instagram isn't the answer. It will only blow this situation up bigger. Gossip is short-lived in the middle school kingdom. Each day has drama of its own. Your daughter won't die of embarrassment over this experience, but she can learn how important balance is. She may keep that dramatic flair, but she doesn't need to be out of control.

Here's something else to think about. No behavior happens in a vacuum. How did your daughter develop her drama queen behavior in the first place? She was allowed not only to have it but to develop it in your home. It might have started even at age 2, when she threw a tantrum and got what she wanted. She may be a naturally expressive person, but over-the-top behaviors would have continued only if she received a reward for them.

The reward she's likely seeking for her dramatic behavior is attention. Those who crave attention but don't know how to get it in a positive way will create a scene that makes them the center of attention. It might have worked at home to get her noticed in the family, but it's deadly among the peer group.

Perhaps at a different time you can have a conversation about *why* she is drama personified. Does she need attention because she feels insecure? Because she thinks the only way she matters in the universe is if she's in the spotlight?

In what ways could she use her attention-seeking behavior in a positive light? Do some brainstorming. Could she join a community youth theater, for example? Liven up the environment of the elderly couple down the block who doesn't get much company? When you focus that natural flair for drama on assisting others and bringing them joy, it's amazing how self-worth can improve.

Just watch and see.

Late-Bloomer Woes

Q: My son Mark is a late bloomer. He still looks like puberty hasn't hit him, even at age 15. When he went to get his driver permit recently, he was mistaken for a grade-schooler. Embarrassing, huh? Especially for a boy. It doesn't help that his dad is a tough-guy military officer.

The kid who used to wrestle with other boys, climb trees, shoot imaginary guns, and strategize war games when he was little has done a shocking about-face. He now hangs out with the skateboarding, "artsy" kids. His clothing and hobbies have changed drastically too.

There's nothing wrong with the new kids he hangs out with—they're great kids. They frequently descend upon our kitchen to graze after school. (Seriously, it's like a herd of cattle storming the place, and no food in sight is left untouched.) I guess my husband and I are just surprised by such a dramatic change.

Every once in a while, I see Mark watching his old neighborhood friends when they hang out together. He seems a bit sad, like he's left out.

Is this normal for high schoolers? Or should we worry that something else is going on?

A: Every person has, at their core, a desire to be loved, to be accepted, and to belong somewhere. This is an even stronger drive during the adolescent years, where having acceptance in a peer group is very important. To adolescents, being accepted *is* being loved. Teens need to find their own group. They often "try on" friend groups like you'd try on clothing. It's a normal, experimental phase.

Your son, you said, is also a late bloomer. That means physically he may not be able to compete with the boys of his own neighborhood. They might look like young men while Mark still resembles a boy. That makes him the odd person out.

If that were you, would you be comfortable?

Well then, neither is Mark. He also probably stares at his muscled, tough-guy father and thinks, *That's what a guy is supposed to look like.* Then he eyes his own four-foot-eleven, 80-pound frame and sighs. *That's sure not me.*

So he gives up competing in that area and looks elsewhere. In order to survive in a peer group, he has to find another one somewhere to belong. That doesn't mean he doesn't miss hanging out with his old friends, though.

Let me assure you that every kid will find his own path. Good thing there isn't only one path in life—there are multiple. At certain times in a child's life, situations change. This is one of those times.

Ask any high schooler about the groups at school, and they'll swiftly categorize them: the druggies, the preppies, the pink-bow girls, the skaters, the nerds. The labels go on and on. Every high schooler is struggling to compete. It might be in art, band, a sport, or anything else in which they find competence and acceptance.

Realize that what your child is doing now might end up being a role he stays comfortable in long-term. Or it might be an experiment that's complete in nine months or even a few weeks.

As a 5-year-old, I wanted to be an ambulance driver. In seventh grade, I wanted to be a dentist. Trust me, you wouldn't want your dentist to be Dr. Leman, DDS. "Oops, sorry, was it a bicuspid or a molar? Anyway, a tooth is out."

When I told the high school guidance counselor about my ambition to be a dentist, he signed me up for Latin. I took it five times and passed it twice.

Next I wanted to be a forest ranger. Why? Because while I was sneaking a smoke out behind the school, I found a matchbook with an ad to be a game warden.

I was clueless. I drifted from place to place because I had two older siblings I thought were perfect, and I couldn't measure up. That's how I lived until I realized there really was a God Almighty who loved me. Then I discovered firsthand that God uses ordinary people to do extraordinary things.

Experimentation is a part of childhood, and that includes clothing, activities, and friends. So allow that boy of yours to experiment in his striving to compete in the male world.

Also, don't worry about his lack of physical development. Every child has his own timeline for that. If his father is well built, your boy has a good chance of ending up that way too . . . even if it does take until the middle of college.

If you can't let your concern go, make an appointment for a routine physical. Privately share your concern ahead of time with the doctor. If nothing pops up during the exam and tests, you'll know there is no reason for any developmental delay, so you can rest easy. Then simply allow the boy to develop at his own pace.

When you see him looking at his old friends longingly, acknowledge that. "I bet sometimes you miss spending time with your old friends, huh?"

He nods.

"Throughout my life, especially with all the moves we've had in the military, I've realized that some friends stay and others leave. I'm just glad you've got an awesome new group of friends." You smile. "Bring them over anytime. I'm so happy to see them."

As long as he is actively living life and enjoying a group of friends, simply keep the grocery cart full and the snacks rolling. It's true: if you feed 'em, they'll come . . . in droves. They'll also grow at their own pace.

Best of all, you'll stay entrenched in that boy's heart because you've remained consistent in his ever-changing world.

They're a Mess after Returning from My Ex's

Q: My ex and I have split custody. Our two girls, now teenagers, live with me during the week and with my ex on the weekends. They have their own rooms at my house but have to share a room at my ex's. Let's just say his rules differ greatly from mine. When the girls get back, they fight like cats and dogs with each other and are surly and snappy with me. Sunday night never passes without one of us crying (usually with a slammed door from one of them somewhere in the process).

How can I turn this *Titanic* around? It's like a bad movie that keeps playing over and over.

A: You're right. That movie will keep playing over and over unless you do something about it. In fact, it's a natural occurrence in homes all across North America when kids visit their other parent and then return home. Chaos reigns. Emotions flare. Why? Because the very act of the switch is a continual reminder that a break happened in your relationship, and now things are different. For those kids, it's as if the divorce happens over and over again.

It usually takes kids a couple of days to settle into their new location. So think of it this way. They're at your ex's Friday night through Sunday night, but it takes them until Tuesday night to settle into your home. Then on Friday they go back to your ex's. That means Sunday through Tuesday night can be h-e-double-hockey-sticks-crazy at your house, and there are only three or so "normal" days for those kids when they truly feel at home. It's hard for anybody to live like that, much less teenagers, who are hormonally charged anyway.

You can't control what happens at your ex's, so don't even try. When your girls are there, he's the parent and they're under his rule. However, you can choose to act differently in your own space to change the equation at your home.

The next time your girls come home from your ex's on Sunday night, be as close to invisible as possible. Post a "Do Not Disturb" sign on your bedroom door. Hide out by yourself and order in pizza. Keep the door locked.

Let those two girls blast each other verbally as much as they want. Endure the noisy fracas for a while. Soon this will dawn on those kids: *Hey, where is the woman who usually referees in our shouting match? She seems to be missing.*

That's when the noise will die down. A dog and pony show is only fun if there's an audience. So they'll come to seek you out. When they do, and you finally open the door, state firmly, "You know what? I'm done with your typical Sunday night behavior. You two make life miserable for everybody in the house. So for a while, when you come home on Sunday, you'll find me enjoying the night in solitude while the two of you work things out. Yes, I can hear you, but I'm not going to get involved. Frankly, I'm disappointed in both of you." Then you shut the door again.

Open mouths will result. The two girls will stare at each other in shock, and likely the fight will dissipate. Sweet, welcome silence will descend upon your home.

The next weekend, the kids will really test you to make sure you mean business. Follow through on what you did before, only this time don't open the door at all. You already told the girls your thoughts once. Believe me, they heard you. Telling them again will only frustrate you. In addition, it implies that they're stupid—since they couldn't process what you said the first time, you have to tell them again. Don't go there. Instead, greet them the next morning at breakfast with a smile.

Is this being mean? No, it's how you can help your kids swiftly come to grips with reality. Yes, there has been a divorce. They live with you now. Dad isn't going to come back. This situation is tough on everybody. In divorce situations, often the kids are thrust into the balancing role. Since the two who usually created harmony in the home—Mom and Dad—are in a mess, the kids feel it's their job to keep their parents happy separately.

But it's not their job. You two are still the adults . . . even if one of you doesn't act like it very often.

Chaos may reign in his home, but stability and security can be your modus operandi.

He Thinks He's a Failure

Q: My oldest child is 17. He's always been the kind of kid who likes to know not only the end game but also the details of what will happen along the way. Rob's smart and wants to be an accountant. He's been intense for months, waiting for college acceptance decisions. When the first college—really hard to get into—turned him down, he fell apart. He cried, saying he was a failure and wouldn't go anywhere in life. He's been depressed ever since.

How can I help him see that this is just one rejection, and that getting into college is one step of a bigger journey? Anytime something doesn't go the way he expects, or his work doesn't turn out as perfectly as he wanted it to, he jumps to the conclusion that he's a failure. He's been that way ever since he was young.

A: Your son is a perfectionist. That's not unexpected for the firstborn of a family, who has had the parental eye focused on him and his achievements. Every little thing is treated as a big deal, so he's been unwittingly trained to be that way. Accounting is a very common occupation for perfectionists. No one wants an accountant who says, "Oh, if we're somewhere in the ballpark, we're fine. Just round up the numbers and the IRS won't mind."

Though perfectionism is great for a career like accounting, being stuck in perfectionism relationally and personally is slow suicide in the long run. You're hard on others and hardest on yourself.

It's time for your son to put his big-boy pants on. He'll need to put in one leg at a time since he's entrenched in his patterns. But now that he's a junior or senior in high school, it's time to suck it up. Life won't always go his way, but that doesn't mean he's a failure.

He needs to face the lies he's telling himself head-on. Not getting into one school among the many he's applied for—and falling apart because he thinks he won't make it in life—is almost laughable, if you think about it. He's a kid who clearly has smarts and skill. He's talented and has worked hard in school. College administration personnel who see his application are bound to take notice. Just because he didn't make it into his first-choice school doesn't mean he won't nail the application process of the other seven schools he applied for.

Do you know what they call even the person who graduates the last of his class in med school? *Doctor.* Same as everybody else.

Right now your son is feeling sorry for himself. He sees himself as counting in life only when he is triple-A and five-star. That's not a healthy view to carry around in life. And he's pulling your chain, trying to manipulate you with his "poor me" antics.

This is a minor disappointment in life. You need to shake up that perfectionistic firstborn for his own good. "No, you didn't make it into your first-choice school," you say. "But neither did another 117,999 kids across the country who applied to be a freshman there this year. You've got seven more schools to go. Just check this one off the list and move on. You see this as a big deal, but to me it's not. It's merely narrowing the focus a little on where you might go." Then you turn your back and walk away to do something else.

Sure, that kid may continue his pity party. But he didn't get what he was workin' ya for—your usual responses:

- You walk on eggshells about the subject.
- "I hate to see you like this. Don't take it so hard."
- "You're really smart. Every other school on the planet would take you."
- "I can't believe that school is so stupid as to not want you."

Instead, you stated the simple facts and then moved on with life. If you deal with the situation that way, your son will move on too. He'll accept the reality as reality.

Somewhere down the road, your daughter-in-law will be thankful for this moment when her perfectionistic husband got a wake-up call. He'll become a better man—one easier to live with.

You can count on it.

Normal Behavior for Grief?

Q: My four kids—14, 9, 5, and 3—recently lost the grandfather they adored. My father lived three houses down and spent tons of time with the kids. Each of my kids is reacting so differently.

My 14-year-old acts like the grandpa he played catch with and who attended all his baseball games didn't even exist. He refuses to talk about him and walks out of the room if somebody mentions Grandpa.

My 9-year-old cries whenever her grandpa's name is mentioned.

My 5-year-old talks about what she and her grandpa used to do as though he's still alive and they're sitting across from each other at a tea party.

My 3-year-old doesn't mention his grandpa at all and acts like nothing happened.

Are these all normal behaviors for grief? How can I keep the memory of their grandpa alive for some and not mention him for others? I can't win, it seems, whatever I try. Help!

A: Kids will react differently based on their age, stage, personality, and relationship with the person who died.

Your 3-year-old is acting his age. He had a warm, loving relationship with Grandpa, but he doesn't have much of a concept of death or what it means. Yes, Grandpa is missing from your dinner table, but he didn't always eat dinner with you. The only thing your young child sees and senses is your sadness and any changes in your behavior. When you told him about Grandpa, what concerned him most was the person he could still see and touch—you.

Your 5-year-old is relating to her grandpa the way she always did, through a shared activity. She doesn't yet know what death means either—that it's permanent. The realization will dawn on her slowly that Grandpa isn't coming over anymore, but because of her age, she will move on without experiencing a deep grief. She, like the 3-year-old, will be more influenced by your pain and sadness.

Your 9-year-old has had more life experience to know what death is, but likely this is the first time it's happened to someone she loves. Her feeling sad is actually a good thing. Tears can be very cleansing and healing, so don't feel bad when you see them. She needs hugs, your love, and little comments like, "Wow, you miss your grandpa, don't you? He loved you so much."

All three of those kids are responding normally.

Your 14-year-old is the one I'm concerned about. Instead of dealing with his sadness, he's pretending not only that he isn't sad but that the man he loved deeply didn't exist. He has retreated inward to deal with his grief without any outside support. Because he doesn't want to talk about it, he'll hold his emotions in, to the point where all of a sudden there will be an explosion. Somebody will pay for that response down the line if you don't curb it now. A shake-up is appropriate, but you have to do it the right way.

Say to your son, "I know how much Grandpa meant to you. His sudden passing shocked us all. He was such a part of our lives, and we're all impacted because he's no longer here." Then explain how each person in the family is dealing with that change. "Your little brother does this. . . . Your little sister handles it this way. . . . You see, people handle grief differently. The one I'm most concerned about is you. People who bottle things up tend to eventually explode.

"You need a way to say how much you miss your grandpa. You wish he was alive today and you could call him on his cell to say hi. That's not silly. You need to be able to say those words without being embarrassed or feeling silly. There's nothing I'd rather hear from you right now than, 'Mom, I miss my grandpa.' If you cry, that's okay. I've cried a lot too. I might even cry with you. Grandpa was a big part of our lives, and he still is because he's in our memories. Part of life is death, and you're choosing to ignore this huge part of life. You can keep saying, 'I don't want to talk about it,' and that's your right. I can't wave a magic wand over your head. But you're missing out on one of the joys of life."

At this point, he'll probably stare at you in disbelief.

"I know what you're thinking. *Just what is so joyful about Grandpa dying?* Well, as you think about Grandpa, you'll realize how important he was to you. That will make you live your life with more passion, enjoying the people around you."

Your son needs a life lesson, and the sooner the better. You don't want him to live like an emotional brick.

You might not have success the first time you talk to him. But you can at least try. If he's not a verbally expressive person, you can suggest he write his grandpa a letter. Most of all, stop tippy-toeing around him. Bring up Grandpa at the dinner table. Let all the kids enjoy telling stories about him. If your oldest gets up from the table, throws his napkin down, and leaves, so be it. He misses part of dinner.

Life in your family can't stop because of one of your kids. You're all in this together. Just because someone died doesn't mean you stop living or stop talking about him. The sooner your firstborn learns this, the better it is for him psychologically, and for your entire family.

Just a Phase Or . . . ?

Q: Shauna has always been happy—the kind of girl people saw as cute and sweet. Then she hit her eleventh birthday. All of a sudden she started dressing differently. She gave away her girly-girl pink clothing she loves, took her allowance, and went shopping at a thrift store for a new wardrobe. Now she varies between emo-type or loose, more masculine clothing. It's a total switch of look and personality. The kids she hangs out with now are very different.

Is this only a phase, where she's trying to reinvent herself or something after losing friends? She gets angry, cries easily, and argues with us now. Lately she's developed a mouth that we don't appreciate when she gets upset.

Is this normal puberty or a warning sign of trouble ahead? Should we be concerned?

A: To quote my dear sweet wife, Mrs. Uppington, whom I have lived with for over five decades—a kindhearted woman who wouldn't hurt a fly—"The 11-year-old female is the weirdest person walking the planet." It's true. All kinds of chemical reactions are taking place in your daughter's body, including hormones and maybe even her period arriving. It's a tumultuous time for girls.

The fact that she changed the way she dresses isn't a big deal. Preteen and teen girls reinvent their look—hair, makeup, clothing— often. These years are a time of experimentation to figure out who she is and what suits her personality best. The good news is that you've reared her with financial sense, at least. Instead of asking you to shell out the cash for her new duds, she used her own money and shopped wisely at a secondhand store. Good for her.

However, in this case she's making a dramatic statement by drastically changing her clothes and her type of friends. Usually there's an underlying reason, and often it's friend based. She might have been dumped or betrayed by her old friend group and is very hurt or looking to get even with them. With the arrival of middle school, there is more pressure on kids to fit in to a group, and maybe she hasn't found hers. She might also be struggling with gender identity if she's switching from a very girly style to a very masculine style.

Now's the time to make an open statement such as, "You seem different these days—worried and upset, maybe. If there's anything going on that you'd like to share, I'm all ears. I won't tell you what to do. I won't judge you. I'll just listen. But if there's something you'd like me to help you with, I'd sure like to try."

Make that simple invitation, and if she doesn't bite, let it go. Even if she pretends she didn't hear you, she did, loud and clear. She'll talk when she's ready.

Part of what you're seeing—the dramatic behavior and changes in dress—is due to living on Planet Middle School. So until you have reason to believe otherwise, don't overthink things.

She used to be the kid who was so sweet that sugar couldn't melt in her mouth. Now she's cranky. Sometimes you merely have to extend grace and let the crankiness go. The testy sensitivity you see can be hormone-cycle based or because she got dissed at school.

If you can't say good morning to her in English without her snapping your head off, try another language: *"Buenos días."* Then smile. After all, you're not guilty of anything except trying to be nice.

When you get that ever-present eye roll, try some humor. "Oh, that was good. Do it again for me . . . in slow motion."

But never put up with a mouth from your kid. That's disrespect, and it needs to be nipped in the bud. The solution is simple. She disrespects you in the morning when she heads out to school and she doesn't get to go where she wants after school. You won't drive her there. If she asks why, tell her, "I didn't appreciate your words or your attitude this morning."

She might hate the lunch she told you she loved and wanted yesterday. Today her clothes are all wrong. It's your fault, she claims, for not washing her shirt. Her hair didn't turn out the way she wanted it to. That's because you didn't buy the right brand-name shampoo.

Everyone has times where life doesn't work out the way they want it to. To feel better about herself, your daughter is working hard to make everyone around her as miserable as she is. She doesn't yet know that won't help her feel any better.

When you're in front of a loaded gun, you can choose to step out of the line of fire. Just removing yourself from the setting usually does the trick. It's no fun to perform without an audience.

Parents are famous for overreacting to their child's wardrobe and hair experimentations. But does it really matter if your daughter's hair is blue for the short while she's into that color? She'll get tired of it or it'll eventually wear off. So what if she wears black lipstick and nail polish for a couple of months? Or if your son insists on buying larger-size jeans so his underwear can peek out the top since that's the current fashion? Simply suggest, "You might want to buy some good-lookin' undies, since the entire planet is going to see them."

It isn't about what your friends think of your daughter's new look. What matters is her heart. She may be into camouflage shirts and army pants at the moment. So what? Is she still rooted as a member of your family? Does she treat her siblings well and her parents with respect?

Nobody is perfect. We all have our bad days. Allow your daughter to have hers, without judgment. But never ever put up with being dissed.

When you're fed up with the changes, remember that it's normal for kids to try different styles on the path to figuring out who they are as individuals, separate from you. Then take a deep breath and remember what you were like at 11 years old—the way you dressed and the stupid things you did.

I used to imagine I was the lead singer for the Beach Boys. I'd play air guitar as I sang "Little Deuce Coupe" in front of the mirror because I thought I had musical talent and the world was waiting for me to share it. The bathroom was my stage.

What I wore out in public at that time was ridiculous, now that I look back on it.

I had already smoked my first cigarette at age 7. By age 11, I'd let a cigarette hang out of my mouth to imitate the cool James Dean.

Whenever I raised a brow at something one of my five kids was doing, a peek back in time did the trick. Nothing any of my kids have done could top the antics my parents put up with while I was growing up.

A little reflection will put the drama in your home in perspective.

She Fears Being Alone

Q: My husband and I adopted Jana when she was 2. After she accepted us as her family, she seemed to "claim" us. As long as one of us was with her, she was okay. But she'd cry even if a good friend came over to watch her for the evening. It took a long time for her to get used to anyone coming and going in her life.

Neither my husband nor I have any siblings or living parents. A month ago, when Jana turned 9, my husband had to have an emergency surgery and died unexpectedly. Jana and I were plunged into shock. Since then, we've become a pair who goes everywhere together. Jana frequently crawls into bed with me. I guess we sleep better by each other's side.

Since her daddy died, she hasn't wanted to go to school. I've considered homeschooling because her fear of leaving me (or of me leaving her?) is so strong. How can I help my daughter over this hurdle? I miss her daddy too.

A: The reason for your daughter's behavior is clear. She's afraid you'll die too and is hanging on to you with everything she has. You are her one sole source of connection and comfort.

When you adopt a child who is 2 years old, fear of abandonment can be a real issue. By that time, 40 percent of your daughter's personality was already formed. In those first two years, when she hadn't met you and your husband yet, she survived in her little world by adapting to her circumstances.

Then suddenly she had a new environment and a mommy and daddy who loved and accepted her with open arms. She learned to trust you. She counted on you being there. She developed a deep bond with you that brought security to her world.

By 18 months of age, children have discovered their ability and power to change or control their circumstances. They can cry on command and throw temper tantrums to get their way. That means she learned early on in your house that clinging to you meant she could control you and make you stay with her.

Clinginess is a very common act on the part of children who fear abandonment. My guess is that when she was little, every time someone came over to your home, she was right behind you, hanging on to your leg. She looked at anyone else who came into your environment as an invader. *Who is this person anyway? He doesn't belong here. This space belongs to Mom, Dad, and me. We don't need anybody else here.*

Only children—even those who aren't adopted—also carry this fear: *What if Mom and Dad die, and there's only me left?* Your daughter's feelings of abandonment are hyped because she's lost her dad unexpectedly.

By age 4, 80 percent of her personality was formed. That included you and your husband in the tight circle of intimacy she allowed. Without you having siblings or parents, you became her everything. Her only family. But the self-sufficiency she developed at an early age made her resistant to accepting other people in her heart. Deep within, she feared losing any people she became close to.

Then suddenly, when she was 9, one of the two people she trusted was ripped away from her. Her fears of being abandoned from age 2 and earlier surfaced in her subconscious because she lost her daddy.

But gluing your daughter to your side isn't the answer. Both of you are individuals, and you need time apart. Counting only on each other in this intense time of grief isn't a good idea. Each of you needs time to heal. You've been through a lot, and so has your daughter. But having your child sleep with you for the sake of mutual comfort isn't healthy for either of you.

Children are all about rituals and patterns. Once they're established, they're hard to break. You should never start a ritual that you can't continue through your child's grade-school education.

Will your daughter still sleep with you when she's 13, 15, 17, 19? Then don't cripple her emotionally so that she thinks, *Without Mom, I can't do anything. I'm nothing.*

Someday you too will die. It's a fact of life. What will your daughter do then if she has learned to rely only on you?

So tonight, for your daughter's long-term health, tuck her into her own bed. Hug her good night. Tell her how much you love her. Then say that each of you needs to sleep in your own bed. "Mommy will always be here for you, but we need our own rooms and some alone time. So I'll say good night now. See you in the morning. It's Saturday, so we can decide together what fun thing we want to do."

Yes, it will be tough. She may whine, cry, or even pitch a fit. She'll sound pitiful, and you'll have to brace yourself. You're the adult here. A slow leak in this situation is disastrous. It's better to force a blowout and get it out of the way. You need to wean your daughter from relying only on you—for her sake and yours. Times of separation are normal, necessary, and healthy.

It also would help each of you to talk to a trusted professional to get through the critical initial stages of grief.

He Only Hangs Out with Girls

Q: My son has always struggled to find friends. It doesn't help that my husband left our family when Sam was only 7. Since then my son has seemed suspicious of any guys—even my well-meaning brother, who tried to step in to take him to father-son activities. Sam has chosen to hang out with girls. He told me once they're "safer."

That was okay when he was younger, but now that he's entering high school, he's getting picked on for only having girls as friends. How can I get my son to see that balance—having both types of friends—could actually be a good thing? Or should I let his friendships play out as they are?

A: My best guess is that your son is wrestling with what a lot of young people wrestle with—gender identification. He may identify and feel more comfortable around women than he does around men. That could be for myriad reasons, including the fact he lost his father when he was young and he's spent most of his time around women.

Interestingly, it's usually the opposite-sex parent who leaves an indelible imprint on the child. Although I was reared by a mother and a father, it was my mother who was continually present in my life. She put up with my numerous antics as a child, stayed calm, and powered on, believing in me despite all the opposition (and there was plenty).

For example, when I was a late teen, I announced at the dinner table that I was getting engaged. I was dirt-poor, working as a janitor making $195 a month. Yet I'd put a $200 deposit down on a ring. Let's just say Jim Carrey doesn't have exclusive rights to *Dumb and Dumber*.

My mom, who'd probably been worn down by my shenanigans, only said calmly, "That's nice, dear. Would you pass the peas?" She had the common sense to take anything I said or did in stride. That incredible quality is one of the reasons I remained so close to my mother all my life, even the times I was the lowest and thought I'd never become anything.

I tested her for years until God finally got ahold of me and I did a 180 in my life. To this day I am much more comfortable talking at a party to a group of women than to a few men. Why? Most likely because my mom was so involved in my life when I was young.

I deeply respected my father, who had only graduated from the eighth grade. He had his own business—laundry—and never made more than 12 grand in a given year. He was always busy and not involved much in family life as I was growing up. After dinner he would find an excuse to go have beers with the boys.

It wasn't until age 56 that my dad became a Christian and did his own 180 in personality and behavior. I then had the incredible opportunity to have a great relationship with him, including a lot of fun, until his death at age 74. Though we weren't close when I was growing up, I was grateful not to have any unfinished business with him. When I think of my father, I know he was far from the perfect man. Yet for a guy with little schooling, he did okay. He managed to take care of his family to the best of his ability.

But your son has been lacking any daddy influence since age 7, so he'd be understandably more comfortable with girls. Encouraging more guy friendships at this point may only frustrate him and make him feel incompetent. Of all the people in his life, you need to understand and support him. He needs your consistent love.

The best thing to do is let his friendships play out the way they are. He seems happy and healthy, and at his age, he should have his choice of friends. Nobody wants their friends picked by someone else. And no high school boy wants father-son activities forced on him, particularly by someone who isn't his father.

In this case, it's best to stay out of the fracas. However, a well-timed comment, if he mentions getting picked on, would be, "I'm sorry that happened to you. The friends you choose are your own business. But keep your options open, Son. I believe in you, and I'll always support you in whatever you choose to do."

If the peer pressure about his friendships really bothers him, he may seek out some male friends . . . or he may not. What he does in that arena isn't important in the long run. What's critical is keeping the conversation flowing between the two of you so his heart is open toward you. Then he can talk to you about anything. You'll have a good relationship with that son of yours both now and in the future.

Separation Anxiety or Something Else?

Q: I have a 3-year-old. Because I'm a single working mom, Katarina spends a lot of time at my neighbor's, who watches her during the day for me. Usually she loves it there, because my neighbor is a stay-at-home mom who has a daughter a little older than Katarina. There's an instant, happy playmate for my daughter, so I don't feel as guilty leaving her.

A week ago when I went to pick her up, though, my neighbor wasn't there. Her younger brother was. Katarina ran for me, crying, as soon as she saw me. Every day since then she has cried and clung to me when I take her to my neighbor's.

My neighbor's the mom of four kids. She says my daughter's probably going through the typical phase of separation anxiety and will get over it. But my mommy guilt and radar are at an all-time high. Is this truly a phase, or is something else going on? This behavior came out of the blue and is so unlike Katarina. How can I reasonably address this with my neighbor and my daughter?

A: Moms are instilled with a keen radar system when it comes to their kids. If your radar is blaring a signal of danger, you're wise to pay attention to it immediately.

Obviously you're between a rock and hard place. You depend on your neighbor to watch your daughter. As a single mom, you're not only bringing home the bacon, you're cooking it too. You need income to stay afloat.

Katarina has been happy at your neighbor's before, but suddenly things have changed. With that behavior on the part of a 3-year-old, I suspect something might have gone on that day that's detrimental to your daughter's health. Before you respond, however, think carefully. What has changed? In this case, the flag of concern is waving wildly. Your neighbor wasn't there when you went to pick her up, but her younger brother was. I'd suspect he's the trigger for your daughter's crying.

Don't ever take chances in a situation where there is a potential pedophile or abuse of any kind. I know this is a tough decision to make. Your job may also be on the line. Making this kind of switch is very inconvenient. However, as a single mom, you know your first response to almost everything in life should be, "How does this match up with my daughter and her needs?"

That means you don't return to that home with your daughter. Now might be a good time for a short vacation to spend a day or two with your daughter and to find somebody else to watch her. If Grandma and Grandpa are nearby and have a good relationship with your child, wonderful! It's time for them to pitch in and help. Or if they live in another state, they might consider visiting your home for a week or two to help with the transition.

What do you do about your neighbor? Since you've had a good relationship with her, it would be wise to have a little conversation. But make sure you have it when you can be calm and loving toward her. In this situation, she may have no idea that something happened in her home to prompt your daughter's fears.

Tell her, "I'm having a difficult time understanding why Katarina is so upset now. She always loved coming here to play with your daughter. But when I picked her up after your brother was here, she ran to me, crying. Now she doesn't want to come here. Since this arrangement isn't working any longer, I've made other plans."

You can't walk in the door and accuse somebody of abuse, but you can at least generate some conversation that may give your neighbor food for thought. Perhaps when you walk out the door, she may think about a few past dealings with that brother of hers. She may put two and two together. No woman wants to believe that her brother could be a pedophile.

This won't help your child, because you won't be returning to that home regardless. However, your loving words may help some other child your neighbor ends up watching. Not to mention that if her brother is a pedophile, then her own daughter is in danger of abuse. Most perpetrators of abuse are, sadly, family members.

So pay attention to that mommy radar. It's usually spot-on. Remember, being a parent isn't always easy or convenient. In fact, the word *parent* comes from the Latin word *parentis*, which means "protector." That's your role, and it's time to play it without backing down.

Suicide Risk or Just Discouraged?

Q: Noah, my 16-year-old, feels like he isn't good at anything. He's not an athlete, not a good student, not a guy that girls like. . . . The negative litany goes on and on. But he stopped me cold yesterday when he said, "I might as well kill myself since I'm good for nothing."

I asked, "What do you mean?"

He shrugged. "What I said." Then he went into his room and shut the door.

I couldn't sleep all night, and I frequently listened at the door to his room. I've kept tabs on him for two days (thankfully it's a weekend, and I don't have to work). Could my son be a suicide risk? Is this a teenage emotional thing or a real cry for help? Should I get a counselor involved?

A: Let's slow down and take things one at a time. First of all, I learned a long time ago that kids sometimes throw things out there to get attention or sympathy because they're bummed out and don't know what else will do. When I was a dean of students at the University of Arizona, I'd often get calls from parents who were sleepless because their son or daughter had called to say how unhappy they were at the university. They painted a bleak picture of what was happening at school and how their child was feeling. Back in those days, when the university was acting *in loco parentis*, I'd call the kid in.

"Hey, Adam, I wanted to talk to you. I got a call from your mom and dad. They're very concerned about you. They said you're having a negative experience at the university and you're feeling depressed. Things aren't working out."

The kid would duck his head and wave dismissively. "Oh, that. I unloaded on them last night. I got a C on a project I thought I aced, and I was really upset."

The bleak picture kids sometimes paint doesn't usually last long. It's a cheap way to get a stroke or a bone thrown their way by their parents.

"It can't be that bad," the parents say, giving their son the opportunity to vent more.

It's like a 4-year-old who says about his drawing, "This isn't any good," and tears it up in front of his mom's eyes. That action is a manipulative setup for her to say, "Now, why do you say that? It's a beautiful drawing!" Behavior only continues if it's encouraged.

I'd tell the worried parents to simply listen to what their student said and not get their blood pressure up. "Don't fall for the 'woe is me' line. Instead, say, 'Wow, sounds like things are rough there sometimes. But you know what? You're a good kid and a tough kid. I believe in you. I know you can overcome this.'"

It was amazing how the nature of the phone calls from students changed when parents followed my advice.

My guess is that right now your son is feeling sorry for himself. He's working hard to get an artificial stroke or hug from you. His words are a cry for attention. For now, allow your son to have his feelings, but don't join the pity party. If his behavior continues—if he continues to be a recluse, not venturing out of his room, not contacting his friends or hearing from them—then you're in tougher waters. Taking your son in to see a trusted professional is a good idea.

You know your son better than anyone else does. Is he working you for sympathy? Is he momentarily discouraged and it'll take a few days to wear off? Or is it something larger, more serious?

If he continues to withdraw or you see any signs of him moving toward taking his own life, act immediately. Make an appointment right away with a professional and insist he go with you. Don't leave him alone for any period of time. As a parent, you are his guardian. His physical safety comes first.

In this situation, your parental gut will come strongly into play. You've seen your son in all types of situations. Does he normally act like this when he's discouraged? Have you seen a repeated pattern develop? Or was his response prompted by an event that will blow over in its emotional intensity, given time?

You, of all the people in the world, know him best.

Abused by Her Boyfriend?

Q: We've never been crazy about my daughter's boyfriend, Jason. They've been dating for over a year, and he has always seemed a bit too controlling. Though they're almost always together, he checks up on Kara when she isn't with him. He even slugged a guy who said hi to her.

Kara insists he's just protective—that he loves her so much he wants to make sure she's safe. She thinks it's romantic, but that kind of intensity scares us. We've tried to split them up, but we couldn't change her mind.

A month ago, on her seventeenth birthday, she came home with a rip in her skirt. She said she tripped. But a friend overheard Jason yelling that her skirt was too short and made other guys look at her. He'd said that she was his and she better not think otherwise.

When I confronted her with what I'd learned, she passed off what happened as her fault for wearing something she knew he wouldn't approve of. She said he loses his temper sometimes, like everybody does. Kara's always been the kind of person who wants to please others and make them happy, even if it hurts her.

Yesterday when I got home from work, pieces of her bedroom lamp were all over her carpet. She quickly said she'd been klutzy and dropped it, but her hands were shaking. My husband and I suspect that Jason broke it and then left.

We're worried, but what can we do? We can't force her to break up with him. We love our daughter, and our parental gut says something is deeply wrong with this "love." We want Kara to be safe.

A: A parent's intuition about their kid is usually right on the money, and you need to trust it. Kara has a pleaser personality, and she's fallen for a controller who is out of control. It's a very typical scenario that plays out in many relationships.

An abuser often has the kind of charming personality that draws a pleaser in unwittingly. His jealous behavior toward other males and his control of her at first comes across as flattering and romantic to her. He reels her in with all kinds of attention and showers her with presents.

Then, once she's within his control and he's removed her freedom without her realizing it, his "personality" changes slowly. His moodiness shows more often. He criticizes her, yells, threatens her—essentially intimidating her and playing mind games. When she's with others, he starts to put her down and embarrass her. All these steps will isolate her further from anyone who could help her. Their arguments increase, but because he's such a "great guy," she thinks it's her fault. She's not good enough and should do better.

Does any of this sound like your daughter and her situation? To me, what you're describing is the classic stage 1 pattern of abuse.

In order for the abuse to continue, there's a very important element that has to remain in place—denial. Right now Kara denies there's a problem with her boyfriend. She claims the responsibility is all hers. It's what *she* did that forced him to rip her skirt, break the lamp, and treat her the way he does. No doubt she's feeling the tension in their relationship. Because of his power over her, she's continually walking on eggshells. Likely when he gets angry, she tries to calm him and reason with him. She sacrifices time with others—even her family—to appease him.

Let me assure you that this type of relationship is not about love. It's about power and control. If you don't step in, he'll have free rein to move to the next stage, where she could be injured physically.

Stage 2 is increased verbal abuse and also physical abuse. He moves from ripping her skirt and throwing the lamp to hitting her. After such an event happens and he sees the bruises, cuts, and other damage he's done to her, he'll cry. He'll say he's sorry. He'll promise, "I'll never do that again." He'll undermine the seriousness of his abuse by adding, "Thankfully, you're not too badly hurt." Then he'll pass the blame. "It's just that I had a terrible day, and I really needed you. But you were somewhere else, and that made me very angry."

Nobody gets angry without their own permission. And hitting someone for any reason is not okay—unless you're an MMA fighter, of course.

She'll stay away from him for a night or a few days until he cools down. Then he'll feel guilty and might bring her a present—flowers or a necklace. He'll reiterate, "It'll never happen again." He'll promise to do anything she wants.

Believing his behavior is a one-time thing, she'll forgive him and make up with him. She'll be happy, thinking they're done with this rough hurdle.

Not so. When he gets his way, he can easily move to stage 3, where he increases the abuse. He might "pretend" to choke her, beat her more severely, or force sex on her. She again tries to reason with him and fights back. She might even threaten to call the police. However, when he says he's sorry, she forgives him and goes back to him, believing he still "loves" her.

Sadly, this cycle repeats itself multiple times. Abuse
stop their patterns. They are endlessly manipulative in
ing their victims that "this is the last time," that they re
change their behavior. But those promises won't be kept. Abusive
controllers continually use a sick combination of psychological
tactics, inducing fear, shame, and isolation.

Your daughter doesn't know it yet, but she needs a loving intervention from the people who love her most—the two of you. Do
it soon. Today if possible. Tell her honestly what you see in the
relationship and what that means from your perspective. Go over
the stages of abuse. Insist she not see her boyfriend or have any
contact with him until she has an appointment with a counselor.
Because you know she'll deny what's happening—she already
has—the very best option would be to pick her up for an "outing," and have that outing be at the counselor's office with the
appointment already booked.

Your daughter will be angry. She might feel betrayed. She
might initially hate your taking control of this situation. But
down the road she'll be relieved you stopped things before they
got worse.

In these cases, it's best if a third party—a professional counselor—
handles walking through what is happening and why it's happening.
You're too emotionally invested in your daughter to see the picture
clearly. She already knows you aren't crazy about her boyfriend.
She might think or say, "You're only doing this because you don't
like him."

When a third party tells her the truth, she is more likely to
believe the scenario. Also, the counselor can help her figure out
why she puts up with and excuses his controlling, abusive behavior.
Understanding why is vital to her future well-being and having
healthy relationships.

This is one of those nonnegotiable hills to stake your flag on as
a parent. The guy she thinks loves her is using intimidating means

to force her to submit to his wishes. You must be immovable in your drive to ensure her safety. That is your first and most important assignment as a parent.

But the next is just as critical for her future. You need to support her as she explores with the counselor why she's fallen for that kind of guy and accepted such behavior. If she doesn't discover the underlying reasons, she will get out of this relationship and right into another controlling one.

Women tend to settle for what they think they deserve. But abuse of any kind is *never* what anyone deserves. It must stop—now.

Your daughter has a right to be loved the right way, and to be loved like that from now on.

Changeable Friends

Q: My teenage daughter found out the hard way how changeable friends can be. The secret she thought she shared with only her three closest friends—which boy she liked—became gossip central on a group chat.

She's so embarrassed, and she feels really betrayed. She says she can never trust anybody again . . . ever.

What can I do to help her get over this hurt?

A: Things could be much, much worse, believe me. Gossip about boys is abundant. Give it a day or two, and the chat groupies will move on to the next hot "potential dating couple" news. Today she might feel like she's dying of humiliation, but she'll feel better in a couple of days. By then she'll either have made up with those friends or dumped them. If there's one thing that's predictable about the teen years, it's that gossip and friendship are as swift and fleeting as a flash of lightning. She doesn't have the life experience to know that yet, though.

Most parents would say, "It can't be as bad as you think." All this does is increase the volume of her wailing. To her, it's the end of the world as she knows it.

Other unhelpful things to say would be:

"Don't worry. I'm sure only a few people know about it." Wrong, since any news of that caliber instantly spreads far and wide.

"There's nothing wrong with liking a boy." But something is terribly wrong with letting him know it. Her embarrassment has made her duck and run for cover every time he's within a mile radius.

For now, she's hurting, and she'll be dramatic about it. Girls usually are, because they're verbal creatures, using 10 times as many words as boys. She'll talk in extremes, using *always* and *never* prolifically.

When she says, "I'll never trust anyone again," the typical parental response is, "You don't mean that."

Don't go there, parent. Actually, at present she does mean that. She has been hurt, violated, and betrayed. The friends she thought were safe ended up sharing one of her secrets. So don't try to paint a rosy picture or wave your magic wand. Neither tactic works with hurting kids.

First, validate how she feels. Her feelings aren't right or wrong. They're her feelings, and they're real. "I'm so sorry that you're hurting. It really does sting when somebody you thought you could trust turns on you." You can also share an experience or two of your own where you trusted somebody else with private information, and it came back to bite you.

Since the situation already happened, you might as well bring something positive out of it—a teachable moment. Continue by saying, "You may not always be able to trust your friends, but you can trust your family. We'll always be here. You can confide in your sister, your brother, your dad, and me."

You may not think she heard you, but she did. She'll reflect on your words in other situations down the road. Next time she might keep her little secrets in the family.

Adolescents are changeable. They change friends as fast as they change underwear. Gossip central is worse because most teens today don't have any filters for what is and isn't okay to post. Once any news is shared in electronic form, it's out there and can't be recalled.

Now that you know what you know, how will you respond the next time your daughter flings herself into the kitchen and says, "I can't go back there—ever! I want to change schools"?

The old you might say in a shocked tone, "What do you mean, change schools? Why do you want to change? What's wrong?"

The new you will say, "Wow, something must be brewing at school for you to say that. If you want to talk about it, I'd love to hear it. If you're not ready, that's okay too. I respect that."

See the difference?

Make your home a calm, safe harbor, and she'll want to return—no matter what kind of day she's had.

We've Tried Everything

Q: We've tried everything with our son, who has been in and out of trouble since he was 11. He's defiant and crass with anybody in authority, even though we didn't raise him to be that way. He's been kicked out of a private school we worked hard to get him into. He only lasted a month in public school before he was expelled for starting a fight.

Last year he was arrested for using drugs. We emptied our savings account and sent him to an expensive rehab. But nothing's working. He only gets more and more angry and deeper into drug usage. He says we can't accept him for who he is.

By that, he means that he thinks he's gay. But he can't be. We're a Christian family, and he hasn't grown up that way. It's just another way that he's rebelling, because he knows it bothers us. For some reason he's trying to get back at us. We didn't do anything to him—all we've tried to do is help him. What else can we do?

A: Your son's behavior is screaming the answer to that question loudly. You've supported him financially and rescued him from the consequences of his actions for years. But you haven't given him what he's longing for the most—acceptance.

He's angry with you because you don't . . . and won't . . . try to understand him. Because of that, he's trying every way he can to get your attention. He doesn't know how to make that happen in a positive manner, so he's acting out negatively by fighting, getting expelled from school, and using drugs.

At their core, every human being is longing for belonging and acceptance. Your son wants you to accept him as he is. If you don't, he'll look for acceptance elsewhere. That includes with his druggie friends. And if he can't find belonging in your home and see it as a safe harbor instead of a place with tumultuous storms of disagreement every time he enters it, he'll seek his belonging elsewhere.

So what can you do? Put aside any feelings you have toward the subject of his sexual orientation. Instead, accept him as he is. No conditions. No judgment. Simply allow him to be who he is—your son.

But that doesn't mean you should continue to put up with his bad behavior or rescue him from the circumstances he caused himself. Love doesn't mean allowing him to run over you because of guilt.

You need to clear the air. Be the adult. Apologize for the way you have treated him in the past. You have no idea how the words

"I'm sorry for not accepting you. Would you forgive me?" can be the tipping point to change your relationship. Start there, then work on the rest. From this point on, he needs to know that you accept him but that you will no longer rescue him from his messes.

If he's arrested again for drug usage, you do the hardest thing in the world. Wait a few hours before you go to the police station. When you get there, don't immediately bail him out. Allow him to stay in the holding cell for a night.

In court, he needs to be the one who stands in front of the judge by himself. You can be there, but at the back of the room instead of by his side. Let reality—the atmosphere of the cell, the police officers, and the stern, unyielding judge—do the talking for you. No lecture from you is needed. Isn't it far better for him to learn a hard lesson now, when he's under 18 and still treated as a juvie rather than an adult?

Stop spending your money. Stop rescuing him. Instead, accept him for who he is and simultaneously allow him to accept the consequences for his actions. That's tough love, and the only way to fly in this situation.

Teased Because of His Weight

Q: Aaron, 11, has always been a bit chubby and has faced his share of teasing. He's seemed to weather it okay, though, since he's had a good friend who's popular and always stood up for him.

Last summer, though, his friend moved away. Now it's hunting season on my seventh-grade son. Every day I can see his head hanging lower when he gets off the bus. Nobody has ever really bullied him physically, so there's not much I can do about it. But I hate to see him get so beat up emotionally. How can I best help my son?

A: Anybody who is different in any way is going to get hammered in the peer group. Your son might be smart, get all the awards, be the star clarinet player. . . . It doesn't matter. Nobody escapes the attention of middle schoolers, who are insecure and can become savage beasts in their drive to be top dog.

It's pretty hard not to have your day in the barrel, so to speak. If Aaron's chunkier than average, he's easy to pick out and pick on. Worse, the only friend who stood up for him is now gone. Your kid's had the rug pulled out from under him.

You can't change the way his peers are treating him. But you can change another part of the equation. Practically speaking, your chubby seventh grader didn't get that way by eating green beans and asparagus. If he's like me, when I go to a restaurant I cut to the chase. I order a bowl of carbohydrates and a bowl of fat grams. I go light on the vegetables.

So let me ask you: who brings the junk food into the house? It isn't the seventh grader. It's usually Mom, who shops at the grocery store and keeps plenty of ice cream, cookies, and chips on hand.

So do what's practical. Give your son the opportunity to eat more healthy foods. Purge the junk from your fridge, freezer, and pantry. Move the whole family toward a healthier diet. You'll be doing all of you a service.

Also, is your son physically active? Is there a sport he's interested in? Could the two of you walk in a park after school or swim on the weekends? Could you invest in a punching bag for the garage or sign him up for tae kwon do?

With a healthier diet and some increased physical activity, your son should naturally slim down. You can't control everything he eats, though. When he's at school or outside your home, he can always find junk food. So how do you instill in him the desire to eat the right kind of food?

That's where a visit to the pediatrician comes in. Call the doctor in advance. Tell her you're concerned about your son's weight and that he's getting picked on at school. She can be a third party to tell him that he's at an unhealthy weight and needs to change his eating and exercise habits. Then she'll insist on a follow-up appointment.

"When I see you in April, Aaron, I'm going to put you on the scale again. I want you to be X weight," she'll say. "It really has nothing to do with the way you look but everything to do with your health. You're carrying too much weight for your height. I know you can do this. I look forward to seeing you in six months." And she'll hand him a list of directives to follow to get healthy.

If a third party who's a respected authority is involved, you don't have to become the nagging, lecturing parent. The doctor will state the facts for you. She'll slip your kid the commercial announcement he needs to hear.

Moving your child toward physical health won't happen instantly. It took years for those pounds to settle in, and they won't come off easily. Furthermore, losing weight and getting fitter won't solve all of Aaron's social issues. However, being healthier will improve his mental and emotional state. He'll feel better about himself, which will help him navigate his world much more easily. It will also give him a more competitive edge for his future endeavors.

That's worth a few inconveniences now, isn't it?

He's Anti-Everything and Doesn't Care

Q: Sean is anti-everything. His actions scream, "I hate you, so don't even try to approach me." The kid who used to skateboard with his friends has become the loner who retreats into his bedroom after school and listens to what my wife and I call "screamo" bands.

When I try to ask him anything, he doesn't respond. The most I can get out of him is a shrug, "Dunno," or "Whatever." He acts like he doesn't care about anything or anyone. He isolates himself from everyone. His old friends don't contact him. His grades have fallen so far we wonder if we should pull him out of regular high school and put him in a trade school. It's like he's lost all motivation. We can't get him to do anything. He's just dull.

We don't know what else to do. Help!

A: Wow. Thanks for the easy question. Whenever you see such dramatic changes—including being a loner, not caring, not contacting friends, and grades slipping—there's a high probability that he's found an unhealthy way to deal with his stress. Your phrase "he's lost all motivation" is a flag for me that he's smoking weed.

Sure, you can drag him to a shrink to see why he's in stuck mode, but my guess is that you'll have minimal success. He's given up. He doesn't care. School in general isn't working for him. Switching to a different school won't improve his attitude.

What you can insist on, though, is a physical checkup. Let the doctor know in advance, out of your son's hearing, that you want her to run a drug test. Share with your doctor what you're seeing. That way she is well informed in advance of the visit and can be the third-party heavy. The results of that test will help you form next steps.

Not choosing to do anything is still choosing. He's playing possum in life. An event might have put him in a tailspin and prompted him to give up. Has something intense happened in your family? The death or illness of a sibling? A divorce and second marriage? If so, some professional counseling might be helpful. Or, as I suspect, he's using drugs and needs a medical intervention.

However, a little shock treatment of your own would be fair. Clearly, he needs a wake-up call. "School evidently isn't working for you. You don't seem to care about it or give it any effort. So it's time to do something different. It's time for you to get a job. Everybody in this family works in order to contribute. I work downtown. Your mom works part-time and does all the laundry, cooking, and cleaning at home. Right now, you aren't doing anything. In order to stay in this home, you are required to contribute.

We'll give you two weeks to search, but we want you to have a full-time job by the end of the month. It takes money to live. While you were a full-time student, we fully supported you. But now it's your responsibility to give back to this family."

He'll probably look at you in shock and then possibly get angry. If so, good. You've accomplished your first goal, which is to at least prompt a response of some kind from Mr. Possum. Part of the reason for his retreat is to manipulate you and your feelings. He shut down so he can get what he wants—attention, even if it's negative.

You shrug. "What you do next is your choice. You can go back to school, study hard, catch up, and make it count. Or you can get a full-time job. You can't live with us forever. Without an education, it'll be tougher for you to get a job. And by the way, now that you're no longer a student, your allowance is suspended. You can make your own spending money."

That sounds so mean, you're thinking. *Clearly the kid is messed up and hurting*. Yes, he is. However, if he is on drugs, where do you think he got the money to buy those drugs in the first place? If he doesn't have a job, he got it from you, his parents. You unwittingly supported his habit.

When his money source is cut off, he can try borrowing from his new "friends." But when he can't pay them back, those friendships will go the way of the dodo bird. Good riddance, in my opinion, since they aren't healthy relationships to start with.

If you want to turn the tides, you've got to be firm. You can't back down. This situation could be more serious than you might think. The longer your kid stays shut down, the more possibility there is that he's depressed.

In today's social milieu, you can't commit anyone to an institution to improve their mental health unless they've harmed someone or themselves. Believe me, you don't want to get to that point. You don't want your kid to be someone who makes the news headlines.

The old adage is true: you can lead a horse to water, but you can't make him drink. Yet you can give him a swift kick in the direction that's good for him.

That's exactly what's needed in this situation.

Ex Is Remarrying

Q: My ex and I parted ways a year ago. We fought constantly so agreed it was best for us and for the kids to divorce. We still see each other because of shared custody and occasionally at family gatherings. On the surface, we get along and tolerate each other.

That relationship got strained further, though, when he started bringing a girlfriend to the family gatherings. All of a sudden my older son started making comments and hatching plans to try to force me and his dad to get together again. Things got really awkward.

Last week my ex-husband announced they're getting married. My son got so angry, he punched his fist through the kitchen window. He yelled, "I hate you! I hate her!" the next time he saw his dad, and he now refuses to talk to him.

I don't like what my ex is doing either—especially so soon after our divorce—but it is what it is. It's his life, and I have my life. We both have to make our own choices. But I can tell my son's really hurting. What can I say and do in a situation like this? It's not like I can change anything.

A: No, you can't change this situation, but you can hug that son of yours a lot more often. Most kids of divorced parents have dreams—which are nearly always unrealistic—that Mom and Dad will get back together. *But this time*, they think, *it'll be perfect. Everybody will get along.*

Your son has had his fantasy blown sky-high by this marriage news. He's understandably angry. However, putting his fist through the kitchen window isn't the answer.

As a mom, you need to have an open, nondefensive stance. "Hey, I can tell you're really going through a rough patch right now. I want you to know that I notice. If you ever want to talk, I'll listen. And just so you know, I'm hurting too. This isn't easy for me either." Such wording builds a bridge of communication through empathy.

Then you add the dash of realism and your support. "You and I don't like what's going on, but we can't change it. Dad will make his own decisions. We'll make ours. But I'll always be here for you. I love you very much and I'm glad you're my son. I'm so proud of who you are."

That son of yours may not talk now, but you've given a warm invitation for him to talk when he's ready. You've also affirmed the kid who is feeling betrayed by a father who would bring another woman to a family event.

When a kid needs some TLC, there's nothing like warmth from good ol' Mom. You can validate his need for belonging, acceptance, competence, and love. A good hug from behind when he's staring out the kitchen window is a great touch. Your son needs to know that his family, shattered as it is, is still a safe place for him.

Your ex should have had enough sense not to do what he's done—bring a girlfriend to a family event and decide to get married. But you can't own what isn't yours. He's no longer married to you.

Do what you can. For example, if that girlfriend is living with your ex, you can pull the plug on your kids visiting. If your ex says, "Hey, wait a minute. It's mandated by the court that the kids have to come," you say, "Well, in spite of that fact, your son doesn't want to come."

That's simple and truthful and asserts your son's right to choose where he lives and visits. What your ex does next is his call. Right now your son needs a mama bear who protects her cub to the utmost of her ability.

Raped

Q: Our daughter, Amy, is 16. A couple of months ago she went to a party with a group of girls. Somebody slipped a drug in her drink. What happened next is fuzzy to her, but she woke up aching the next morning in a hotel room she didn't remember going to. Flashes of the previous night hit her, and she vaguely remembered having sex with multiple boys. She started shaking and vomiting, then passed out. A hotel staff member found her and called 911, and she was taken by ambulance to the hospital.

My husband and I had been frantic all night, trying to track down a couple of the girls we knew. Glen finally got a call from the hospital midmorning, when Amy was coherent enough to tell them our phone number.

When we saw our daughter, she was trembling and fearful—very unlike Amy. My husband was furious. He pursued going after the boys with the police. The resulting investigation over the next weeks revealed the culprits. We were even angrier when we discovered this wasn't a first offense for two of the boys. We're still continuing the legal battle to this day.

If I could turn back time, I'd make sure this event never happened. Amy used to be playful and adventuresome. Now she's reclusive and stays at home instead of going out with friends. I've caught her doodling, "It's my fault . . . all my fault." She jumps at noises, refuses to wear anything except thick sweatshirts and sweatpants, cries easily, and sleeps wrapped in a thick blanket even in the heat of summer. She refuses to see any of her friends and doesn't want them to know what happened to her. She'd rather cease to exist in their lives than have them know she was so stupid, she says.

My husband and I are intensely concerned about her and the impact this traumatic event will have on her life. What else can we do?

A: You're doing all the right things in this terrible situation. You *should* go after those young men legally with everything you've got. It won't change what happened to your daughter, but it may save some other girl from becoming their victim. It will also show your daughter that you believe what happened to her and that you fully back her.

What happened *wasn't* consensual since Amy was drugged and sex was forced on her, but a victim of rape always feels guilty. She wonders, *What could I have done differently? Did the way I dress make them do that to me?* A victim thinks that the rape was her fault, that she "asked for it."

Rape is not about sex. It's about power—power over someone weaker than you. It's not a mistake. It's a crime. That's why you have to go after those boys. Sadly, such crimes are not unusual today. With the male drive to compete as top dog, a lack of control, increased testosterone in the teenage years, and alcohol and drugs mixed in, anything can happen. And it did—to your daughter.

Amy needs a thorough physical checkup. I know she had one at the hospital, but some aftereffects may not show up until later—in her blood work, for example.

How your daughter is responding is normal for trauma victims. Like soldiers who return after battle, she flinches at noises. She's also dressing in a way that camouflages her body so nobody will see that she's a girl with a figure. That's because she still thinks she holds some responsibility for what happened.

Your daughter needs assistance from a rape crisis center or a counselor who has dealt with survivors of rape. She needs an outsider who can help her wade through her feelings and the aftereffects of that experience.

She also needs some loving instruction that will help her feel safer in the future. We all can command our feet where to go. We can walk into situations that could be dangerous and unhealthy—such as parties where alcohol and drugs are clearly involved—or we can take a pass and choose to do another activity that doesn't carry as many inherent dangers.

This experience will stick with Amy. She needs your love, support, understanding, and listening ear as she heals. Pushing her to go out and spend time with friends isn't the answer. Getting her some professional help is.

What she needs to know most is:

- The rape wasn't her fault. It was a crime that happened to her, against her will.
- You are working to ensure that the perpetrators pay for their crimes.
- It's normal to feel helpless, guilty, angry, scared, and embarrassed . . . and much more.
- You will always be available for her if she needs and wants to talk.

You already did one of the best things you could—immediately went to the hospital as soon as you found out. That one act means more than you will ever know because it cements your concern and love for her firmly in her mind.

Abused Kid Now Beats Up Others

Q: I'm trying hard to love my stepson Mark, who is now 14. My wife's previous marriage was a rough one with an abusive husband. After ending up in the hospital a couple of times, she decided she had to get out of the situation—if not for her own good, then for her son.

By then Mark was 9 years old. His most vivid memory, he told his mom once, was when his dad threw her across the room and

Mark heard her back hit the air conditioner, kicking it on. Awful, huh?

We married last year, after several years of dating. She was understandably cautious. I was happy about at last providing a stable home for Mark. But he's gotten worse. Now he's become the kid who hurts those who are littler and weaker and even takes on older guys who outsize him in a fight. The pattern of beating others up and getting beat up keeps repeating itself.

My wife and I are worried about him but feel helpless. I feel so bad about the way he had to grow up but don't want him to end up like his dad. Ideas?

A: When you grow up watching and experiencing physical violence in your home, you'd think it would repel you. However, the terrible reality is that, if the abuse is commonplace, kids can become almost anesthetized to it. It happens so often that they actually get used to it. It becomes a common, "comfortable" situation.

Think about it this way. Let's say you have an old T-shirt that's tattered and almost falls apart when you put it on. It doesn't look good to anyone else, but you're used to it and it's comfortable. So you continue to wear it because it's part of your comfort zone. You identify with it. Life wouldn't be the same if you didn't wear that shirt.

Abusive behaviors are horrific, but the cycle can continue because the victims and perpetrators get used to it. That's why people who are abused can easily become abusers themselves down the road.

Mark grew up in a home where his mom was treated as lower than an animal. Every time that happened when he was young, it reinforced his developing worldview that she as a woman was merely on earth to absorb her husband's wrath, ridicule, and poor treatment. Because his mom had been so belittled and beaten down, she accepted the treatment as normal for a period of years. By allowing it, she conveyed to her son, "I'm not worth it. He can say and do anything to me and I'll just take it. It doesn't make any difference."

Often abused women stay in relationships for financial reasons or because they think it'll be better for the kids. But her not saying no and staying with her abuser until Mark was 9 showed him a pattern of negative behavior toward women in general. Also, his mantra of how he would treat others developed: *I only matter if I'm tough and strong and can dominate others . . . like my dad. Otherwise, I'll get eaten alive.*

Although Mark hated what his dad did to his mom and how his dad treated him, it was familiar. He got used to it. When he grew older, likely he said the same things as his dad. He also did some of the same things as his dad—like beating other people up.

But he also now feels unconsciously guilty for his behavior, because he remembers his mother's pain—that memory of her back hitting the air conditioner. So he allows himself to be beat up because dealing with the physical pain is better than the mental pain of recalling the memory.

What can you do? You can psychologically disclose for Mark what you think is going on. Pull him aside, man to man. "I know life has hurt you badly. As a result, you're angry and you want to hurt others. You also feel guilty for not being able to protect your mom, so you want to be hurt. Neither behaviors are healthy ways to live, and they'll destroy your life down the road. I care too much about you to let that happen. So here's what we're going to do."

You outline the plan, which includes counseling for what has happened to him in the past. And if he continues picking on other kids and fighting, the repercussions will be real and instant. He'll be pulled from the activities he loves to do, like the track team. He won't be able to game with his buddies on Friday nights.

Mark will test you to see if you mean what you say. You stick to the plan and never waver. Then you conclude by saying, "Now is the time to make a change. I believe you can do it, that you're powerful enough to change your behavior. The next time you have the urge to hit somebody, I want you to think, *What do I usually do? What will I do differently this time?*"

I know that's a tough assignment for anybody. Because Mark's behavior patterns are ingrained, it's like telling an alcoholic not to drink or a druggie not to shoot up. Striking back at someone else verbally or with his fists has been Mark's immediate high. So he needs something else to replace that fallacious adrenaline rush.

There's a distinct difference between the average male and female when they feel angry, upset, or sad. Males will tend to fight back physically. They'll hit each other or punch walls. Females will tend to cry or lash out verbally. They'll slam doors. However, as society is changing, it's now becoming more common for girls to go after each other physically.

Helping Mark learn how to deal with his anger now, at 14, is critically important for the safety of everyone in your home. That includes your wife and any younger children you might have. As he bulks up to become a young man, his growing size will make him even more powerful . . . and a potential threat with his abusive tendencies. He has no track record of being kind to women. He didn't see that quality patterned in his own father.

What he needs most is a firm, no-nonsense, loving encourager who believes in him enough to urge him on toward behavioral change and hold him accountable for it. You can be that for him since you are the new person in the equation.

Will it be easy? No—he'll hate you sometimes. Yet you already knew stepping into this marriage and instant fatherhood wouldn't be easy. It's just been a tougher transition than you'd imagined. But the stakes are high, and every effort you put in now is extremely important not only to Mark but also to the welfare of your entire family.

A Diet Craze ... or Anorexia?

Q: My 13-year-old daughter is constantly on her phone, watching YouTube videos about her favorite stars' lives. She's almost fanatic about it.

In the past year I've noticed she's eating less and less at meals and seems to comment a lot about how "fat" she is (she's five foot three and weighs about 115 pounds!) compared to every other girl. She's adopted a lot of crazy diets lately—insisting on eating only lettuce with no dressing. When I tell her she should get more protein in her diet, she gets mad at me for "controlling" her life too much. We end up at an angry impasse.

I'm seriously getting worried because her size 3 clothes now hang on her. But I can't make her eat. What now?

A: No, you can't make her eat, and yes, you have reason to be concerned. If this had happened only once or twice—where she felt like she was fat and had to go on a diet—I would say it's a typical young teen phase. However, this behavior has happened for a year, and the diets she adopts seem to be getting more extreme. No growing girl can exist on lettuce.

Also, note the word *controlling*. Girls who suffer from anorexia (eating very little or nothing) and bulimia (binge eating, then vomiting to purge their overeating) feel controlled by others. They feel like they have no control over anything in their life except for their eating, and that's why they focus on it. They often have perfectionistic moms or dads who plan out their life for them and expect them to follow that road map. They feel they can't make any decisions of their own.

Those with eating disorders have a myopic view. They don't see themselves the way we see them. You notice your daughter getting skinnier by the day. She may look in the mirror and view herself as fat.

Although your daughter is already making comments about being too fat, she's hardly fat at her height and weight. However, anorexia and bulimia aren't really food issues. They're *control* issues. Often kids who develop these illnesses are perfectionists. They are detail oriented—likely she's already researched her favorite stars' height, weight, and BMI and is trying to match them. If an actress says she eats only two apples a day to maintain her best look on camera, your daughter will try that. She's likely keeping records—on her phone or in her head—of every calorie she eats.

At her age, your daughter's body is changing significantly. She may just have gotten her period. If she eats too few calories, not only does she get skinny, but she can throw off her body's natural rhythms and hormone cycles. When the body doesn't get enough food, it stores calories as fat, which takes longer to digest. Ironically, by starving herself now, she is increasing her risk that she may gain weight more easily once she's an adult.

Anorexia and bulimia (as well as cutting) are illnesses that have to do with control and perfectionism. They are serious and can lead to all types of physical ramifications. If not curtailed, anorexia can lead to death. Singer Karen Carpenter's death was the first highly publicized death from anorexia that I can remember. It was a tragic wake-up call to a lot of parents whose young girls were struggling with that very issue.

You can't deal with your daughter's behavior by yourself. You need to hightail it to a medical specialist who deals in eating disorders. Depending on the extent of your daughter's illness, she may be able to overcome it with counseling, or she may need some rehabilitation. In-care centers such as Remuda Ranch exist for that very purpose. Do some research and take action to get your daughter help immediately.

Karen Carpenter was a beautiful, talented woman. The struggle with perfectionism and control that led to her eating disorder wasn't noted as a serious issue until her destructive patterns had already been set. Then it was too late for anyone to help her change her mind-set.

It's not too late for your daughter. But she needs your loving intervention to be physically, mentally, and emotionally healthy.

TOP 10 PRINCIPLES FOR HANDLING LIFE'S HURTS WELL

1. Realize that feelings are not right or wrong. They're simply what your child feels.
2. Acknowledge the hurt and the reason for the grief—the elephant in the room.
3. Tell the truth in a straightforward, loving way instead of providing a la-la land experience.
4. Remember that children grieve differently than adults.
5. Don't promote a victim mentality that will shape your child's worldview negatively. Instead, approach hurting and injustice as a learning experience.
6. Teach your children when to endure, stay, and fight, and when to run away for their own safety.
7. Provide an always-listening ear and a nonjudgmental heart.
8. Give your child age-appropriate ownership of the solutions.
9. Be a realistic champion and encourager. Tell your child, "Rough things happen in life, but I believe in you. You can rise above this situation."
10. Focus on growing a loving, supportive parent-child relationship. If your children are safe and secure in your home, they can overcome nearly anything tossed their way.

NOTES

Chapter 1 "Out There" Issues

1. Trace William Cowen, "14-Year-Old Girl Dies in Crash after Sister Livestreams While Driving Drunk," Complex Life, July 25, 2017, http://www.complex.com/life/2017/07/woman-livestreams-car-crash-killed-sister-instagram.

2. "Teens Filmed, Laughed While Man Slowly Drowned, Authorities Say," Fox News, July 20, 2017, http://www.foxnews.com/us/2017/07/20/teens-filmed-mocked-and-laughed-while-man-slowly-drowned.html.

3. Glen Kwon, "Why Aren't We Talking about the Latest School Shooting?" *Huff-Post*, April 12, 2017, http://www.huffingtonpost.com/entry/why-arent-we-talking-about-the-latest-mass-shooting_us_58eef70be4b0156697224c71.

4. Kory Grow, "Sixteen People Die Falling through Grate at South Korea Concert," *RollingStone*, October 17, 2014, http://www.rollingstone.com/music/news/sixteen-people-die-falling-through-grate-at-south-korea-concert-20141017.

5. "Sexual Assault and Rape," Joyful Heart Foundation, accessed July 25, 2017, http://www.joyfulheartfoundation.org/learn/sexual-assault-and-rape?gclid=EAIaIQobChMI68u4rfin1QIVSWt-Ch1zFg1hEAMYASAAEgJM_PD_BwE.

6. "Segregation and Integration in America," accessed July 25, 2017, http://www2.dickinson.edu/departments/amos/mosaic01steel/Marie/sia.html.

7. Josh Eloge, in discussion with the author, July 25, 2017, Ashville, New York.

8. "Are You Prejudiced? Take the Implicit Association Test," *The Guardian*, March 6, 2009, https://www.theguardian.com/lifeandstyle/2009/mar/07/implicit-association-test.

9. "Family Abduction," National Center for Missing & Exploited Children, accessed July 21, 2017, http://www.missingkids.org/theissues/familyabduction.

10. Jessica Klimczak, "Author Spotlight: Hannah and Josh Eloge," *Blurb*, March 2016, http://www.blurb.com/blog/author-spotlight-hannah-and-josh-eloge/.

Chapter 2 When Hurt Hits Home

1. Richard Pérez-Peña, "1 in 4 Women Experience Sex Assault on Campus," *New York Times*, September 21, 2015, https://www.nytimes.com/2015/09/22/us/a-third-of-college-women-experience-unwanted-sexual-contact-study-finds.html.

2. Louise Saunders, "When Two TV Greats Meet: Oprah Winfrey Opens Up on Her Traumatic Childhood during David Letterman Lecture Series," *Daily Mail*, November 27, 2012, http://www.dailymail.co.uk/tvshowbiz/article-2239102/Oprah-Winfrey-opens-traumatic-childhood-David-Letterman-lecture-series.html.

3. Oprah Winfrey, quoted in Saunders, "When Two TV Greats Meet."

4. "Males and Eating Disorders," NIH Medline Plus, accessed July 27, 2017, https://medlineplus.gov/magazine/issues/spring08/articles/spring08pg18.html.

5. Edwin Arlington Robinson, "Richard Cory," Poetry Foundation, accessed July 27, 2017, https://www.poetryfoundation.org/poems/44982/richard-cory.

6. The basic principles of the four goals of misbehavior are taken from Rudolf Dreikurs and Margaret Goldman, "Adlerian Child Guidance Principles," Alfred Adler Institutes of San Francisco & Northwestern Washington, accessed July 21, 2017, http://www.adlerian.us/guid.htm.

7. Monica C. Worline, quoted in Skip Prichard, "Awakening Compassion at Work," Skip Prichard Leadership Insights, May 8, 2017, https://www.skipprichard.com/tag/awakening-compassion.

8. Trudy M. Johnson, quoted in "Feelings after Abortion: Post-Abortion Syndrome," LifeFacts, accessed July 27, 2017, https://www.lifesitenews.com/resources/abortion/abortion-risks/feelings-after-abortion-post-abortion-syndrome.

Chapter 3 The Three Basic Fears and Their Antidotes

1. Kevin Leman, *Have a New Kid by Friday* (Grand Rapids: Revell, 2012), 70.

Chapter 4 Why Grief Serves a Purpose

1. Dreikurs and Goldman, "Adlerian Child Guidance Principles."

ABOUT DR. KEVIN LEMAN

An internationally known psychologist, radio and television personality, speaker, educator, and humorist, **Dr. Kevin Leman** has taught and entertained audiences worldwide with his wit and commonsense psychology.

The *New York Times* bestselling and award-winning author of over 50 titles, including *The Birth Order Book*, *Making Children Mind without Losing Yours*, *Have a New Kid by Friday*, and *Sheet Music*, has made thousands of house calls through radio and television programs, including *FOX & Friends*, Hallmark Channel's *Home & Family*, *The View*, FOX's *The Morning Show*, *Today*, *Morning in America*, *The 700 Club*, CBS's *The Early Show*, *Janet Parshall*, CNN, and *Focus on the Family*. Dr. Leman has served as a contributing family psychologist to *Good Morning America* and frequently speaks to schools, CEO groups, and businesses, including Fortune 500 companies and others such as YPO, Million Dollar Round Table, and Top of the Table.

Dr. Leman's professional affiliations include the American Psychological Association, SAG-AFTRA, and the North American Society of Adlerian Psychology. He received the Distinguished Alumnus Award (1993) and an honorary Doctor of Humane Letters degree (2010) from North Park University; and a bachelor's degree in psychology, and later his master's and doctorate degrees, as well as the Alumni Achievement Award (2003), from the University of Arizona. Dr. Leman is the founder and chairman of the board of Leman Academy of Excellence (www.lemanacademy.com).

Originally from Williamsville, New York, Dr. Leman and his wife, Sande, live in Tucson, Arizona, and have five children and four grandchildren.

If you're looking for an entertaining speaker for your event or fund-raiser, or for information regarding business consultations, webinars, or the annual "Wit and Wisdom" cruise, please contact:

Dr. Kevin Leman
PO Box 35370
Tucson, Arizona 85740
Phone: (520) 797-3830
Fax: (520) 797-3809
www.birthorderguy.com
www.drleman.com

Follow Dr. Kevin Leman on Facebook (www.facebook.com /DrKevinLeman) and on Twitter (@DrKevinLeman). Check out the free podcasts at birthorderguy.com/podcast.

RESOURCES BY DR. KEVIN LEMAN

Nonfiction Books for Adults

The Birth Order Book
Making Children Mind without Losing Yours
Have a New Kid by Friday
Have a New Husband by Friday
Have a New Teenager by Friday
The Way of the Shepherd (written with William Pentak)
Have a New You by Friday
Have a New Sex Life by Friday
Have a Happy Family by Friday
Planet Middle School
Education a la Carte
The Way of the Wise
Be the Dad She Needs You to Be
What a Difference a Mom Makes
Parenting the Powerful Child
Under the Sheets
Sheet Music
It's Your Kid, Not a Gerbil!

Born to Win

Sex Begins in the Kitchen

7 Things He'll Never Tell You . . . But You Need to Know

What Your Childhood Memories Say about You

Running the Rapids

Becoming the Parent God Wants You to Be

Becoming a Couple of Promise

A Chicken's Guide to Talking Turkey with Your Kids about Sex (written with Kathy Flores Bell)

First-Time Mom

Step-parenting 101

Living in a Stepfamily without Getting Stepped On

The Perfect Match

Be Your Own Shrink

Stopping Stress before It Stops You

Single Parenting That Works

Why Your Best Is Good Enough

Smart Women Know When to Say No

Fiction: The Worthington Destiny Series, with Jeff Nesbit

A Perfect Ambition

A Powerful Secret

A Primary Decision

Books for Children, with Kevin Leman II

My Firstborn, There's No One Like You

My Middle Child, There's No One Like You

My Youngest, There's No One Like You
My Only Child, There's No One Like You
My Adopted Child, There's No One Like You
My Grandchild, There's No One Like You

DVD/Video Series for Group Use

Have a New Kid by Friday
Making Children Mind without Losing Yours (parenting edition)
Making Children Mind without Losing Yours (public school teacher edition)
Value-Packed Parenting
Making the Most of Marriage
Running the Rapids
Single Parenting That Works
Bringing Peace and Harmony to the Blended Family

DVDs for Home Use

Straight Talk on Parenting
Why You Are the Way You Are
Have a New Husband by Friday
Have a New You by Friday
Have a New Kid by Friday

Available at 1-800-770-3830 • www.birthorderguy.com • www.dr leman.com

Kid-tested,
parent-approved

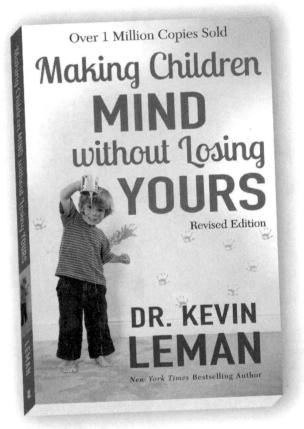

Over 1 Million Copies Sold

Making Children
MIND
without Losing
YOURS
Revised Edition

DR. KEVIN
LEMAN

New York Times Bestselling Author

If anyone understands why children behave the way they do, it's Dr. Kevin Leman. In this bestseller he equips parents with seven principles of reality discipline—a loving, no-nonsense parenting approach that really works.

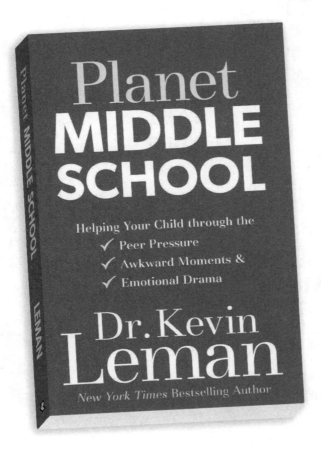

New York Times Bestselling Author
Dr. Kevin Leman
Will Help You with Real Change

Use these easy action plans to improve your communication and life in five days!

Understanding the power of
your birth order can
CHANGE YOUR LIFE.

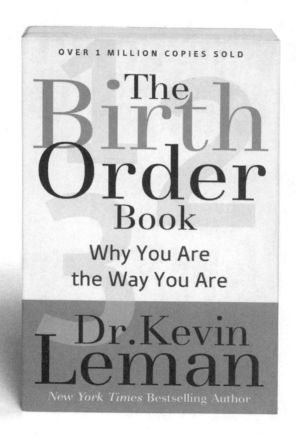

Let Dr. Kevin Leman show you how.

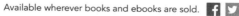

Powerful kids don't just happen...
THEY'RE CREATED.

Whether loud and temperamental, quiet and sensitive, or stubborn and manipulative, powerful children can make living with them a challenge. But it doesn't have to be that way.

DO YOU WANT THE BEST POSSIBLE
EDUCATION FOR YOUR CHILD?

In this practical book, parenting expert and longtime educator Dr. Kevin Leman takes the guesswork out of choosing the best school for your child. He explores the pros and cons of public, private, and charter schools, as well as homeschooling and online schooling, in order to show you how to find the education that fits your child's unique needs.